VISIONS
IN THE NIGHT

By

NATHANAEL EDWARDS

Visions In The Night

First Edition

ISBN 978-1-7394260-0-2

Authors notes:
1. All scripture quoted in this book are from the
English Standard Version unless otherwise stated.
2. All persons mentioned in this book are done so
with their permission.

Contents

Dedication

I want to begin by thanking those that have been such a great support in helping me bring this project to completion.

Life Community Church Storrington, I feel truly honoured to be chosen to serve God among you. You have always blessed and supported me and my family. In 2022 you allowed me to take a sabbatical that enabled me to finish this book. Thank you to the leaders and the congregation for your love and support to me and my family.

To my Mum and Dad, John and Doris Edwards, I would not be the man I am today without you. Dad, you have instilled in me a zeal for the Word of God and Mum you have led me to pursue a life of compassion and care for those in need. I hope I have managed to combine the best of both of you. You are my parents but you are also my role models. Thank you both for everything you have given and taught me.

Barbara Workman, you are a Godsend. I had taken this book as far as I knew how. I had been praying for someone to help me bring it to completion. I will never forget how excited I felt the day you told me that God had instructed you to help me. I will also never forget how my heart sank when I received back the first draft with all the notes, indicating where the book needed amending. It took me some time to get the courage to begin the process of rewriting, but your guidance was amazing and I am forever indebted to you for your time and support.

Michael Simbeye, thank you for working with me in the ministry, some brothers come by natural birth and there are others that come through the work of the Holy Spirit. You are my spiritual brother and I love you as much as if you were my natural brother.

Finally, I want to dedicate this book to the most important people in my life, my wife and three children.

Katherine, you are all that I could have hoped for in a wife, you cover my weakness and shame, you release me to ministry without complaining, you honour and encourage me and you take care of me. More and more I believe God made us for one another. I'm not sure anyone else would have put up with me like you have. Thank you. I love you.

Zion, Levi and Taya, I am so proud of all of you. You are kind, compassionate, caring, wise, God-fearing, funny and obedient children. I couldn't have asked for more delightful children. Thank you for letting me travel away from home. I know it can be hard sometimes not having Dad at home but I know God will reward you for sharing me with others. I love you all.

Finally, Jesus my Saviour and my Lord. I am overwhelmed that you would use a fool like me. I so often feel inadequate in all that you give me to do. Thank you for not giving up on this stubborn child. Your love has won me and I am yours now and evermore. You are my everything. I love you.

Forward
By Michael Simbeye

I first met Nathanael in the early 2000s. I was a young teenager then and little did I know that later in the years to come our friendship would escalate into something beyond my understanding in serving God through countless projects. Together we have helped widows, vulnerable people, young children and built a powerful ministry. We have worked and gone on missions together, prayed together, cried together, faced challenges and laughed and I have had the privilege to be alongside him and watch his ministry grow from strength to strength.

Nathanael's teaching of the word of God is so simple and straight forward and he has a unique gift on how he reads and understands Gods word and just believes it. He has a gift of faith, he believes what he reads from the word and I have seen so many things happen as a result of his faith. Every time he teaches, he doesn't complicate the topics, and this has been the most rewarding experience of my life because I have learnt so much from him and he has helped me become the person I am today. His influence on me comes from how he handles himself and the word of God and inspires and challenges me to dig deeper into God's word. I love his love for the work of God, he is a man who has so much compassion for others and always wants to do more for others. He is a selfless soul.

In the early days of our friendship, we were preaching together, he was speaking and I was translating for him in a youth camp in Zambia. After listening and translating his message, I knew within me that he was called to serve because it was the first time in my life that I heard such a pure and concrete teaching of the gospel.

My faith has grown and developed massively as a result of our teamwork and many times when we walk side by side whether in Zambia, Uganda, Rwanda, Malawi or the United Kingdom, any- where where Life Community Churches are, Nath- anael is a man who speaks his mind about some- thing and is confident that he will someday see it happen. When he speaks, his words do not come out as a command or a directive, but as a story told to a friend of a goal that is possible to achieve. Almost everything we have discussed and wanted to see come to fruition, has come to pass, which is why I call him my 'Secret Prophet' as I have seen the hand of God on his life.

Of the many memories that I share with Nathanael I remember one day we were on a mission trip to

Malawi and we were in the deep villages in Southern Malawi where living conditions were a challenge. Rooms were crowded and small, dust and dirt surrounded us and we were invited to sleep on the hard flat floor of the room. For me being a Zambian, I am familiar with these conditions, but I was worried for Nathanael, him being a European, that he wouldn't be able to cope but as I saw how Nathanael managed to survive, I realised then what an incredible man I was working with. Nothing bothered him; he was fine with everything and made no complaints. He handled himself like a man who was used to sleeping like this all his life and this reminded me of Jesus and his disciples when they were doing ministry, as the son of God did not care about whatever conditions they would find themselves in. Their focus was to preach the gospel, to set the captives free and to introduce the kingdom of God to everyone they met. Having that experience with Nathanael on that mission trip, taught me about how humble he is and what a loving, compassionate, and respectful heart he has for others.

One time we were walking on Eden Farm in Zambia and he stated; "One day there will be a church here on the farm" and he was pointing to a place on the farm that was total bush. As I looked at him I could feel that what he said would come to pass, but in my heart I knew it would be a big challenge as we didn't have any resources or leaders to make it happen. However, three years later the church was built at the farm, and I am in the leadership team of the church which became the birthplace of Life Community Ministries in Africa. Currently we have seven churches in Zambia, eight churches in Malawi and two churches in Mozambique, with a new branch about to open in Uganda, plus the church in the UK. We all work closely as a network of churches. All this as a result of that first conversation as we walked.

Another time, five of us, all good friends of mine and Nathanael's, were praying together. Nathanael shared a vision about starting Life Community Ministries which became the church network ministry we are now all part of. As we were praying about this, I also had a vision: We were in the mountains and we were walking together and when we looked behind us we saw a great multitude of people following us on the same path. We came to a big mountain cliff and we knew where we wanted to go, because we could see the other mountain ahead of us, but there was a great cliff and a deep valley that was impossible to cross. In that vision I asked Nathanael "What are we going to do? We cannot go back and we cannot go forward, we are trapped!" Nathanael looked up and he said: "We have to look to Jesus for he is the way and he will give us the way we are looking for." So, we started praying on top of the mountain with everyone who was there. We prayed and prayed and when we opened our eyes, a miracle had happened. We were not on that mountain anymore, we found ourselves on the other side, on the mountain we needed to be on. Not just us but everyone we were with had moved. We looked back to where we had come from and said to one another, "What has just happened?" In that moment, everyone was joyfully praising God.

As we finished praying, I knew exactly that the vision of Life Community Ministries, which Nathanael had shared, came from God and would come to pass, and so it has, and is still expanding. In the few years of running this ministry we have hosted powerful conferences, seminars and ministry training schools. I have seen miracles, healings, provision provided, lives transformed, and visions and goals achieved, prophesies fulfilled and the power of the Holy Spirit working in the lives of God's children.

When we face inevitable challenges in limited resources for the work of God, Nathanael always quotes Psalms 50:10-12,

> *"for all the animals of the forest are mine,*
> *and I own the cattle on a thousand hills".*

He ends by saying "there is room for more".

This all happens with him because he hears and obeys the voice of God. His heart and love towards

God's people is just so awesome! I have learnt so much personally from Nathanael. My spiritual life and my understanding of the word has developed massively because of Nathanael's influence on my life.

This book has personally taught me so much and I relate to everything within its pages. I believe his words will change your lives too, because these are real stories of his experiences, the revelations God has given him, the prophesies he has had and speaks of his personal relationship with God.

This book exposes the power of darkness and how it is possible to deal successfully with sin and fear, temptation and pain, not only exposing the power of darkness but providing light, comfort and revelation. I believe and trust that this book will challenge you, direct you where you need help, encourage you and give you the desire to do more for God because we all have a greater capacity for more in God's kingdom. So be ready!

God is still speaking...

Michael Simbeye

1. Introduction
The reason for this book

It was 1995 and the year of my first ministry trip with Bunty Bunce, an itinerant missionary supported by my home church, New Life Christian Centre in Croydon, England. I was 16 years old and excited to serve God in missions. We had arrived in Auckland, New Zealand after spending two months teaching in churches throughout Asia and Australia. God had been moving powerfully in our meetings and we had a sense that we were ministering under an open heaven. One night in a time of prayer I felt The Holy Spirit bring to my mind the words of *Matthew 19:21* where Jesus spoke to the rich young ruler and instructed him to, *"Sell all you have and give the money to the poor."*

I had an immediate sense that God was telling me to do the same thing and I was quick to inform Him that he definitely had the wrong man! I was far from being rich, if I had indeed sold all that I had, it would only have amounted to about £50. "How is £50 going to help the poor?" I asked myself. I was willing to do as God was asking, it was no great sacrifice to me, but it just didn't seem to make sense. I'll admit that I began to question if

God was actually speaking to me but I just couldn't forget this word.

God reminded me of this verse several times over the following months, often I would be praying and that one line would come to me again and again; *"Sell all you have and give the money to the poor."*
"OK Lord, I will, if that's what you want me to do", I prayed, but still it just didn't sit right with me. Unlike the rich young ruler in the passage, who wanted to serve God but was too afraid of a life without wealth, I had no riches so giving away my possessions would be no sacrifice and very little benefit to the needs of the poor.

Looking back now I don't know why I didn't seek God more fervently to understand what he was saying to me. Maybe it is because I was so focused on the small glimpse of what He had allowed me to see, that I was unable to step back and see the full picture. If only we would take the time to seek God and silence our own minds, we would hear much more from him. It wasn't until I returned home about three months later, that I finally understood what God was saying to me. It is possible that God kept me from seeing the full picture to cause the meaning of the words to have a deeper impact. After arriving home from the ministry trip, I was in a time of prayer when this same verse came to me again, *"Sell all you have and give to the poor."* I began to feel frustrated. "Lord, I don't have anything to sell!", I said. "Why do you keep bringing this scripture to me?". I felt the Holy Spirit responding to me, "you have much, look at what I have given you." Suddenly my mind became clear, God wasn't referring to my material possessions; he was talking about the treasures he had put in my heart.

As a child, and into my teenage years at school, I struggled with learning to read and write. I was unable to write my own name until I was about 11 years old and I was diagnosed with dyslexia when I was 13. At the time dyslexia was still not widely recognised and most schools had no provision for children with learning difficulties. This meant that I found it hard to achieve academically. A reading test I had taken before my exams at age 16 revealed that I still only had the reading age of an 8 year old.

Not only did I struggle with reading and writing but remembering details like names and dates was almost impossible. Even today after reading through the bible many times over I still struggle to recall in which books you will find different scriptures. Thanks to my parents, not being able to read and write had no effect on my self esteem. I knew I wasn't unintelligent but I didn't know why I just couldn't learn like other children did. Growing up I never thought it possible for me to be a teacher of God's word, as I was unable to study well. Reading anything was difficult, reading the bible was near impossible. However, as I'm sure you know well, God chooses the foolish things in this world to shame the wise and the weak things to shame the strong (*1 Corinthians 1:27*). God isn't restricted by our lack of ability; when we are weak, He is strong, and through our weakness He is glorified. So, God, who knew my failings, knew exactly how to use me in spite of them. God knew that I was not able to study His word in my own ability but still He opened opportunities for me to teach and preach. In the natural I was not qualified, but He is the God of the supernatural. Over the years as I was unable to read and study God's word fully for myself, God taught me many of the lessons of scripture through spiritual dreams and visions.

That night in my prayer time, I finally realised what the Holy Spirit had been saying to me, it was these dreams that were the treasures that God had given me and God was telling me to sell them and give to the poor.

I still had a problem. I was 17 and had left school a year earlier with a U (ungraded) grade in English. However, in obedience I began to write down my dreams as best I could, keeping them in a book to use when the right time came. Reading them back many years later, I find it hard to understand what I had written but God has caused these dreams to have such an effect on me that I am able to remember most of the detail without much prompting.

Three months later I embarked on my second missions adventure to Chingola, Zambia to support Ben and Brenda Pitout, another mission partner of my home church. About a week or two before I left, the wife of one of our Elders came to me with a word from God. She prophesied over me that while I was in Zambia, God was going to teach me to read. On the back of her words, I packed lots of books. Sure enough over the next 4 months I slowly developed the ability to read clearly. This was without a doubt a work of God. I could now finally read the bible without struggling. My writing and spelling was still very bad but praise God, I could read fluently and I knew it was a miracle.

After returning from Zambia I enrolled in an evening class to retake my English GCSE exam. I finished with A marks in all my course work as well as an A in my speaking and listening. My final grade was a C due to spelling and punctuation mistakes in my written exams. To think that just two years earlier, my work was so unintelligible that the examiners chose not to grade my work, awarding it a U for ungraded and now I was awarded a C grade. I had no one on one tutoring, just the Holy Spirit, my bible, and a pile of good books. Thank you Jesus! This was one of many little miracles that has led to the writing of this book being possible.

Not long after, Bunty Bunce invited me to accompany her and a friend from the US on a second ministry trip. I prayed and sought God as to whether I should go or not. I had no clear answer and felt unsure as to what I should do. Not wanting to make a wrong decision, I asked some of the Elders in my church for their advice. Two told me that they felt I should go, and the other two told me they felt I should stay. After receiving such great spiritual counsel, I was none the wiser and there were only a few weeks left for me to make a decision. I prayed about it again and this time I felt God respond, "You choose, Nathanael, but if you go you will have to preach."
...Decision made.
"O.K. I won't go", I said.
"Why not?", I felt God asking.
"I am not able to preach, I have nothing to give", I replied.
"I have given you many things to teach, remember your dreams." I felt God responding.
Suddenly my mind changed, "OK. I will go". Somehow I felt empowered by the fact that God had given me messages to share and this knowledge changed how I felt about the opportunity of being a witness for him. Often we are scared to speak out for God because we feel inadequate but in reality God delights in our inadequacies as it means that we have to depend on Him. What an

honour it is to speak as a messenger for God, to proclaim His words and His thoughts. Whenever we feel that we are too weak, too small or too unschooled then that is the very moment that we can say, "it has to be God, I have nothing to give." So many times I have been in that place and then been shocked at what comes out of my mouth. Jesus told His disciples in *(Luke 12:11-12)*

> *"And when they bring you before the synagogues and the rulers and the authorities, do not be anxious about how you should defend yourself or what you should say, for the Holy Spirit will teach you in that very hour what you ought to say."*

For the first month or so of my trip I had few opportunities to speak in meetings, but I used my time to write down my dreams along with a few scriptures, so that I was ready to share when the time came. One Saturday morning two months into our trip, while we were in New Zealand, I received a phone call from, one of the Elders of my home church back in the UK, to tell me that Bunty's mother had fallen very ill back in England and suggesting that Bunty return home immediately. There was concern that Bunty's mother would not last much longer. Bunty was out shopping when the call came, so I got on the phone and booked her a flight home that same night. By the time she returned home from shopping to the time we left her at the airport seemed to be like a matter of minutes, though I am sure it was really some hours. It wasn't until we returned home that night that we realised we had two church services booked for the following morning, followed by three weeks of speaking engagements at camps and church meetings throughout New Zealand.

My friend from the US and I decided we would preach at one meeting each the next morning. As I sat in my room preparing, there was a knock on my door. My friend had come to say "Nathanael, I feel the Lord is saying you are to speak at both meetings tomorrow." At any other time, I think I would have responded that if God told me the same thing then I would do so, but I knew she was right. The next day I spoke from my dreams and some passages from the Bible to back them up. I'll never forget how that morning in the first meeting, I watched as 4 old ladies (who made up almost the entire congregation) sat and wept as I spoke. I was amazed at how the dreams God had given me could be such a blessing to these women. At the end of the second meeting with a much larger congregation of a few hundred, a line of people queued to speak to me after being touched by the message. That morning I really understood what it meant to lean on God and to speak out the words he had put in my mouth. From a child I had received many prophetic words about being a preacher and teacher of God's word, but I had felt disqualified by my limitations. God's Spirit is able to work through all His creation. Over the coming weeks my American friend and I spoke in meetings, taught leader's retreats and led holiday clubs all over New Zealand. Once again God did another little miracle in both of our lives by empowering us beyond our years and experience.

As time has passed and I have been able to study God's word more fully, I am always so encouraged and excited at how the truths that God revealed to me in dreams have lined up with His word. They have remained with me all through the many years and been a great reminder to me that God is always speaking; that He wants us to know the truth of His word and that nothing not even the inability to read can hinder the truth of God's word, from being revealed to us, his sons and daughters.

I was only 16 when I first felt God had told me to write this book and I am now in my mid 40s. I have tried many times to complete and release it but each time, something has prevented me from finishing. Finally it is done. I realise as I read through old drafts that there were many things that I still needed to learn before it was ready. The truths were always there but I had to learn the depths and the weight of them. Of course I am still learning but I believe now is the time to make this book available.

I have sought in each chapter to set the context in which I received my dream. Then to share the dream as I received it and explain its immediate application. Then I have sought to offer a wider application and how I have found this same truth in scripture. Finally, I have finished each chapter with a prayer and a summary of the key points to help with personal application.

In this book are some of the dreams God has given me. I share them out of obedience because I believe God has told me to do so. I pray that through each one of these dreams God will speak to you as He did to me, that you will be encouraged and built up in your faith, taken on to new heights in His love and purpose for your life.

As God showed me all along through (*Matthew 19:21)* that I should sell what I have and give to the poor, much of the money made from this book will be given to help the work of Life Support and Life Community Ministries. Both Life Support and Life Community Ministries are organisations that I have the great privilege of being involved with. You can find out more about them in the back pages of this book.

So here they are: the dreams that I believe God wants me to share with you. I hope they speak to you as they did to me and that you put this book down with a renewed vision and understanding of God's love for you and that you will develop a greater passion to see His kingdom come on the earth. My prayer is that what God has encouraged and challenged me with will also encourage and challenge you, that when you have finished this book you will have a greater love for Christ, for pursuing his presence, for his church and for the lost.

2. Why Dreams?
Why write a book of dreams?

I often joke that God speaks to me most in my dreams, because it is the only time He can get me to be quiet, stay still and listen. Although this is said in jest there is some truth in it. In my case, God wanted me to learn some spiritual lessons at a young age and he knew I would not be able to discover those truths through reading the Bible because of my reading difficulties, so he made sure the message got to me in a way that would shape my thinking and that was through my dreams.

I was baptised in the Holy Spirit when I was 7 years old and from that time on I began to operate in the gifts of prophesy, words of knowledge and speaking in tongues. I often saw visions whilst praying and from a young age had been involved in praying for people for deliverance. Thanks to my parents and the church I grew up in, I was encouraged to be sensitive to the voice of the Holy Spirit and had no problem believing that the Holy Spirit wanted to speak to me and to others through me.

It is the work of the Holy Spirit in our lives that brings us into greater relationship with God the Father. We, as followers of God, are not left alone to find our way in this world but rather as Jesus promised, His Spirit comes into our lives and works in us to bring us into a deeper relationship with the Father.

In *Joel (2:28-29)* God says

> *"And it will come to pass afterward that*
> *I will pour out my Spirit on all flesh;*
> *your sons and daughters shall prophesy,*
> *your old men shall dream dreams,*
> *and your young men shall see visions.*
> *Even on the male and female servants*
> *in those days, I will pour out my Spirit."*

The point here isn't that God only speaks to young men in visions and old men in dreams, but rather that God will speak to men and women this way by His Holy Spirit poured out on their lives. God has said he will pour His spirit out on us all. He wants to speak to us in creative and impacting ways. God in his awesome wisdom knows how to speak into our lives in ways that will mean something significant to us.

Being a very visual person I love to see maps and plans drawn out in front of me so I can picture the plan or the route. God (of course) is fully aware of this, so he knows how to speak to me in a way that will make me sit up and take note. For me that has often been through dreams and visions. God does also speak to me in other ways; I can remember many times where people have given me words from God or prophesied over me. I have been deeply moved by the spirit of God speaking to me through His word. All of these different ways God has spoken to me have left an impact on my life, however, if you ask me to tell you the words of prophecy people had spoken over my life, I would have to look for them on scraps of paper in my Bible or somewhere on my laptop. The sermons that so moved me and impacted my life still bear fruit today, but if you ask me to repeat the content of the sermons, I would struggle to remember what was said. God's written word is different, it is living and I remember what it says even when I can't recall the exact scripture and verse. The dreams God has given me are also different. I can tell you exactly what happened in each dream and what it meant without checking any notes. Apart from scripture I can say the most impacting and memorable messages I have received from God have been through my dreams. I believe the fact that I can remember these dreams so clearly after many years is evidence that they really were given by the Holy Spirit.

In the Bible there are many accounts of God speaking to people through dreams, giving direction or promises for the future. Daniel was known for his gift of interpreting dreams, which led to him becoming a great leader in Babylon. Joseph, who's dreams led to him becoming the prime-minister of Egypt, (Genesis 41:37-44) both received dreams for himself and interpreted dreams for others through the power of the Holy Spirit. Another Joseph, the husband of Mary, Jesus' mother, was also spoken to in dreams on at least three occasions. The first one we know of was when an angel told him that the child Mary carried was God's son and that He would save the people from their sins (*Matthew 1:18-21*). Later, an angel appeared to Joseph in a dream and told him that he should flee to Egypt with Jesus and Mary (*Matthew 2:13-14*).

Just think about this for a moment. The life of the son of God, Jesus the Messiah, the one on whose shoulders the salvation of the world depended, was threatened by King Herod, a crazy, bloodthirsty tyrant, who would stop at nothing to make sure his rule was unchallenged. He even ordered the murder of every boy under the age of 2 in Bethlehem and the surrounding area. Now God, in His infinite wisdom, chose to warn Joseph, not by an audible voice, nor by an angel speaking to him face to face, nor by a visiting prophet, but rather in a dream. The Bible doesn't say why God spoke to Joseph in this way. All we know is that He did and Joseph listened. Joseph didn't question that the dreams were from God, he believed that dreams were a way that God spoke to his people.

He knew the stories of what God had done and how he had spoken in times past, and he knew to pay attention to these dreams. God chooses to use dreams to communicate some of the most important things he wants to say. God is still speaking through dreams today; we need to be careful not to dismiss dreams as unimportant but to be attentive to what God is saying to us. As a child I remember in church that people would often share visions and dreams that God had given to them. I have always been thrilled to hear how the Holy Spirit speaks a word to someone that is intimate and personal to them. Put simply, the Holy Spirit speaks my language and He speaks yours too.

Dream Interpretation
The gift of interpreting dreams is clearly seen in scripture and there is great fruit when men and women of God are used to make clear to people the meaning of dreams. One danger I see in the church today though, is that it is becoming a habit for some Christians to seek out dream interpreters to make their dream clear to them. This may sometimes be necessary but I am convinced that if God gives you a dream he will generally give you the gift needed to make the meaning of that dream clear to you. There is a biblical precedent for God's people to make known the meaning of a dream to someone who is not a follower of God, such as Daniel & Nebuchadnezzar, or Joseph & Pharaoh, but I would always encourage Christians to ask

God for the meaning of their dream, rather than looking for an interpreter. Of course this doesn't mean that this would never be necessary, just not the norm. I would question why we ask others what God is trying to say to us, rather than waiting on God to reveal what he wants us to know. Often I have shared dreams that God has given me with other believers who have taken it on themselves to try and interpret my dreams for me. Their subsequent interpretation is normally vastly different from what God has shown me that the dream meant. Several times people have asked me for the interpretation of a dream they believe God has given them. Each time I have told them to pray and ask God what He is saying to them. I have found that generally the person already knows or very quickly discovers what the dream means. If for some reason God doesn't reveal the meaning of the dream, then it is possible that the interpretation is not yet meant to be known. Sometimes God speaks to us to prepare us for something He wants us to understand at a later time. On such occasions it is a good idea to write the dream down and keep it for a time when God reminds us of it.

It is wise to wait before making radical decisions based on our dreams, remember that God is patient and kind. He will always bring confirmation if we ask Him. It is also wise if you are learning to be led by the Holy Spirit to check what you feel He is saying to you with a mature Christian friend or leader who is used to hearing from the Holy Spirit.

So many people in their passion to please God, can be hasty or over excited and end up making costly mistakes. God has given the church men and women who are endowed with wisdom, and it is good for us all to learn to listen to others who have walked paths before us. Always remember though that God is gracious and compassionate. If we get things wrong, He is ready to pick us up, brush us down and set us back on track.

Warnings about dream interpretation.
One crucial principal in dream interpretation is to ensure that what you believe a dream means is in line with scripture. God will never guide us to do something or teach us something in a dream that is contrary to scripture. Dreams that are inspired by the Holy Spirit will be confirmed as we read the bible and submit to its wisdom.

I was once in a church meeting and the speaker was talking about dream interpretation. They told the church that, if you dream in colour then your dream is from God and if you dream in black and white it's from the devil. I was a bit shocked at this statement, maybe it was true for them personally but it is most certainly not true for us all!

In pursuing God for dreams and dream interpretation we should be careful not to follow fads and other people's ideas. The spirit of God speaks to us all differently according to our gifts and personality. How He speaks to me in dreams won't be the same as how He speaks to you. Once in a meeting I heard a speaker say that if a dog appears in your dream, it represents something evil. This is ludicrous. If I were to dream of a snarling dog that wanted to eat me then I would know it represented something evil, but if I dream about one of my pet dogs, past or present, that would represent something completely different to me. When it comes to interpreting dreams we need to be careful that we don't get caught in religious superstition which really is like a form of occultism. There are books written by Christians on how to interpret dreams, laying out all sorts of ideas on what different imagery may represent. While I am sure there are some things that can be learned from observation we must be careful not to attribute to the Holy Spirit ideas that are presumptuous or superstitious.

The same image in two different dreams can mean completely different things. For example I have had two dreams in which a lion has played a central role. In one the lion represented the devil, in the other it represented Christ. If, after the first dream I had drawn the conclusion that every time I saw a lion in my dream it represented the devil then I would have missed the meaning of the dream in which Christ was the lion. We also need to be careful we don't try and interpret spiritual dreams through our intellect alone. We are not trying to understand the workings of the mind but rather to understand what is being said by the Holy Spirit.

Some people have recurring dreams because there is some issue in their life; often these issues can be discerned by listening to them sharing their dreams. We can ask people about their dreams to try and understand what may be going on in their lives. I have no doubt that this is useful and can give real insight, but it is not the same thing as interpreting dreams. This type of dream may not be a message from God, but rather our minds processing and revealing what is going on in our lives and bringing out suppressed fears and hurts. Through observation we can learn much about what dreams are revealing and we should learn in this way but this observation only goes so far. It is the Holy Spirit that reveals the hidden things and often imagery in dreams is very personal to the individual that has had the dream. So observe and learn but don't set hard and fast rules. Rather be led by the Holy Spirit and listen to Him for understanding, He can reveal to us the meaning of people's dreams.

We also need to be careful of assuming all our dreams are messages from God. It is perfectly normal for our minds to be active at night and such activity can produce very peculiar dreams. Maybe like me, you have a vivid imagination or maybe you ate too much cheese before you went to bed! I often have very vivid dreams but there is something different about a dream when it comes from the Holy Spirit.

Holy Spirit or Overactive Imagination?

As a young man learning to hear from God in dreams, I could have become a little over zealous expecting that every dream was a message from God. I remember one night I dreamt that I was sitting on a toilet without any clothes on. Suddenly I looked over my shoulder and realised I was on the stage in my church and the whole church was sat behind me watching me. I was so embarrassed and ashamed but couldn't move. As I woke a thought entered my mind. "People are going to see your shame and you will be humiliated in front of the church". I felt sick at the thought but it only took me a few seconds to bring myself into the presence of God and immediately I was able to recognise that's not from God. He doesn't lead us into shame but he covers our nakedness. Had I been falsely super spiritual in that moment, I could have been brought into fear but fortunately I knew my God and I knew that he leads us into freedom not fear.

Checking the source

There are some ways we can tell when God has given us a dream. For me, receiving a dream or vision from God has a deep impact on my spirit; I wake with a feeling that this is not just another dream, it is significant and very real. I can clearly remember what was said and done for some time after waking up. I sometimes wake with a strong awareness of the presence of God. My response when I have this experience is to write down my dream and then to pray and ask God what He is wanting to say to me. I also ask that if this dream is not from God that I would forget it. I then wait for God to speak to me. Over the days, weeks, months and in one case even years, the Holy Spirit begins to reveal to me the meaning of the dream.

My dreams have been a clear way for God to speak to me. However, I have always weighed up what I feel God has said to me against scripture. I have never found that I was misled or confused in my faith by my dreams. Scripture must always be held as the highest authority, above our own opinions, feelings or imaginations.

Whenever I have asked God for the meaning of a dream that I knew He gave me, God has always responded by showing me the meaning. I have never needed someone else to interpret my dreams for me. Wisdom comes from godly counsel and it is always a good idea to ask for the opinion of godly men and women especially when we feel led by a dream to make big decisions. I have often shared the things I feel God is saying to me with people I know hear from God. Allowing spiritually mature people to test what we believe God is telling us, is always a wise step. As I said, when I am asked to give an interpretation to someone else's dream, my response is to ask them what they feel God is saying to them. Most times they already have a very clear understanding of what the dream means. I am happy to ask the Lord and see if he will give me the meaning of their dream, but I would rather they heard from God themselves. I will pray for them that God shows them the meaning and listen to see what he says, even if I believe I have the interpretation; I would rather they hear themselves before I share what I believe God is saying. How much better is it for someone to realise they have heard from God than for them to believe that they have to come to someone else to hear from him.

When we have a dream that impacts us, it can be hard to know for sure if the dream is from God or not. I have listed the following questions that can help us determine if a dream is from the Holy Spirit or not.

1. Are you left feeling impacted?
When I receive a dream from the Holy Spirit, the dream affects me in an emotional and spiritual way. The feeling I have sticks with me throughout the day and often into the coming days. I can't just ignore the feeling, I have to do something about it. Other dreams can affect me emotionally too, but I find within a short time of waking the feeling passes.

2. Are you drawn to spend time with God?
After receiving a dream from the Holy Spirit I of-

ten wake with a desire to draw near to God in worship or prayer. I feel hungry for Him and I feel a need to listen to Him.

3. Does the dream stay with you?
The events of the dream don't fade away as dreams normally do. The dream remains vivid. I am often reminded about the dream as I sit and think or lie down to sleep the next night. The dream even comes back to me in the day long after I have woken up.

4. Are you left with a sense of God's presence?
I wake up with a sense of the nearness of God. This can be waking up with a joy or peace in my heart or with a sense of awe.

God speaks through dreams
God is speaking to mankind, calling the lost to himself and revealing his ways to his children. He has given us the word of God to guide us, but that's not all, He has also given us the Holy Spirit. The Holy Spirit speaks and leads us. One of the powerful ways he does so, is through dreams.

On a ministry trip to India in 2008 I had the privilege to speak to around 50 teachers at a school in a town to the north of Calcutta. The teachers were a mixture of Hindus, Catholics and evangelical Christians. I shared on how they are called to sow seeds into the lives of the children they are teaching and that with the right conditions the seed would grow into a great harvest. I shared Jesus' story of the Sower and how some seed fell upon good soil. I encouraged the teachers to help their students cultivate their lives to be good soil and challenged the teachers to do the same in their own lives, explaining that the words of Jesus are good seed for our lives. As part of my talk I also shared a dream that God had given me along with its meaning. At the end of the meeting it was a joy to pray with teachers Christian and Hindu alike. One of the woman teachers came to talk to me, she said she had been moved by hearing how God had given me a dream and then revealed its meaning to me. She shared how she had had a dream a few days before and that she felt very strongly it had been from God. She asked if it would be OK to tell me what the dream was. Excited to hear what God had said to this lady I listened carefully. "In my dream" she said "I was praying at my altar in my house where I have idols. I pray at my altar each night. As I was praying my idols fell down in front of me and smashed to pieces on the floor." She went on. "Next I saw myself putting my hands on peoples' heads, as I did so they began to scream and shake; evil came out of them. What does it mean" she asked. "What do you think it means?" I said. "Well" replied the teacher. "I think maybe God is telling me that I shouldn't be praying to idols, just to Him. When I saw the idols falling down I didn't feel scared or upset but happy." I told her that the Bible teaches we should not pray to images but to God alone. "What about the second part" I asked. "I believe God wants to give me a gift to cast out evil spirits" she replied. "That's great" I said. I showed her *Mark (16:17)* where it says,

> *"And these signs will accompany*
> *those who believe:*
> *in my name they will cast out demons;*
> *they will speak in new tongues".*

The teacher was very excited, not just because God had given her a dream but because she had also received the interpretation from Him. All I had done was to confirm, with scripture, what she had already received from the Holy Spirit. I led the teacher in a prayer of commitment to Christ as her only God and she renounced her idol worship. A friend and I then laid hands on her and prayed that God would release her in the gifts of the Spirit and specifically in the gift of deliverance. "What are you going to do now?" I asked. "I will go home and smash my idols" she replied. This woman didn't need me to interpret her dream; she just needed confirmation that what she felt God was saying to her was true. I strongly believe that when God gives you a dream, if you seek Him, He will show you what He wants you to know.
It is great to have people in the church with the gifting to interpret dreams. We need prophets. We need all the gifts of the spirit but we need those that function in these gifts to help others to hear

from God themselves not build their own ministries, so that only they can speak out the words of God. I am more and more convinced that the most effective ministry in church is that which reproduces itself and releases the church to move in that same gift.

This example of God reaching out to an Indian woman in her dream is not unique, there are many testimonies of people finding salvation in Christ because they had a vision or dream in which Jesus or an angel appeared to them. I have met several people from a Muslim background that have become followers of Jesus through dreams. I remember how one young man that came to speak at our church shared how in a dream he had seen Jesus calling him to follow Him. This young man had to leave his whole family to do so. Once again, we see that God chooses the medium of dreams to reveal himself to people.

Dreams can help us to see things that words alone can't convey. Often in a dream you feel that you are part of what is happening. Dreams aren't like a story you are reading or a play you are watching, but rather they are more like an event you are living. In a dream or a vision, your mind, spirit, emotions and to some extent your whole body are involved. The sights, sounds and feelings can be very real. To me dreaming an event is second only to living it. What better way is there for God who made us to experience life through our minds, body and spirit, to reveal himself to us.

It is worth noting that just as God desires to build us up, warn or direct us through our dreams, so also the devil desires to mislead and confuse us through our dreams. I don't say this to bring fear but to remind us that we must weigh up what we feel is from God and not assume that all dreams having an impact on us are from God. I once had a dream about a friend of mine and in the dream his wife died in a car crash. As I woke I was hit by how real my dream was and for a moment I wondered If God had given me this dream as a warning. What should I do, I wondered? I felt like calling my friend to warn him but I stopped and quieted my heart before God. Immediately I had a sense that this was not a dream from God. That moment spent waiting on the Holy Spirit, may have stopped fear and manipulation from the devil getting a hold on me, and more importantly my friends. We are not meant to judge spiritual things just with our intellect but with the Spirit. God has given us His Holy Spirit as a gift so that we can weigh up the things that we download through our dreams and thoughts. So seek God for the meaning to your dreams and take time to understand what he is wanting to teach you. Be patient, maybe the answer will come over time. What a joy and privilege it is to have God speak to us. Let us not despise this spiritual gift but use it as it was meant - to build up ourselves and the church, the bride of Christ.

As you read this book you may be reminded of dreams you have had in the past or you may find that God begins to speak to you through your dreams. Let me encourage you to write down what you feel God shows you, even if at first it doesn't make sense. A time may come when the dream becomes clear and you will begin to under-stand that God had been preparing you all along.

3. The White Lion
A Call To Holyness

Romans 6:1-12

*"What shall we say then? Are we to continue
in sin that grace may abound? By no means!
How can we who died to sin still live in it?
Do you not know that all of us who have been
baptised into Christ Jesus were baptised into his
death? We were buried therefore with him by
baptism into death, in order that, just as Christ was
raised from the dead by the glory of the Father,
we too might walk in newness of life.
For if we have been united with him in a death like
his, we shall certainly be united with him in a
resurrection like his. We know that our old self was
crucified with him in order that the body of sin
might be brought to nothing, so that we would no
longer be enslaved to sin. For one who has died has
been set free from sin. Now if we have died with
Christ, we believe that we will also live with him.
We know that Christ, being raised from the dead,
will never die again; death no longer has dominion
over him. For the death he died he died to sin, once
for all, but the life he lives he lives to God. So you*

also must consider yourselves dead to sin and alive to God in Christ Jesus. Let not sin therefore reign in your mortal body, to make you obey its passions."

I remember having what I would call 'spiritual dreams' from a young age. Most of them were very personal to me and helped to inform my understanding of God and His heart toward me as a follower of Jesus. The first dream that I remember discerning to be a message to the church and not just for me personally is the one I want to share with you first. I received it when I was about 15 or 16 years old.

At the time in our church, we had a large youth group. Our church was a big church by British standards with over one thousand members at the time. Our town of Croydon is a borough of London and larger than many cities in the UK. We were truly a city church and this meant that we had quite exciting opportunities as a youth group. We went on mission trips, hosted concerts and even got involved in leading church services. There was a feeling among us that our group was something special and I remember conversations questioning if there was a better youth group anywhere in the country. We were a nice group of young people that truly cared for each other and desired to be pleasing to God, but we were becoming slightly arrogant and proud of the fact that we had such a large group of young Christians. From a young age the church had encouraged us to be led by the Holy Spirit and to pursue spiritual gifts. Many of our young people had exercised spiritual gifts and had known the presence of God in their lives. Something seemed to have changed though and I was beginning to feel we had begun to lose our way, it felt that our attention was shifting from devoting ourselves to God to being more concerned about our talents and abilities.

————

One night I dreamt I was sitting in a small meeting room in our church's building; The room is at the back of the building, where functions often take place. It was a youth meeting night and the room had around 40 young people sitting on chairs in a circle. The circle was broken up into smaller semi-circle groups of about 5 or 6 youths talking amongst themselves. I saw many of my friends sitting together just enjoying each other's company and chatting over the events of the week. Our youth group always felt a safe and warm place to be, full of excitement and expectation and this night in my dream was no exception.

Suddenly my attention was drawn to something in the centre of the room. Walking around the groups, I saw a beautiful white lion. The lion was large, much larger than a normal lion. He was powerfully built with a beautiful white mane and he was perfectly groomed. As the lion walked round a small group of friends in one corner of the room, I noticed that they stopped talking to each other and became more and more focused on the lion and less aware of each other. Before long the group's focus was drawn completely to the lion, who seemed to feed on the attention they were giving him. Everyone in the group was now talking to and stroking the lion as if he were a pet cat. They were no longer interested in their friends but all their attention was completely taken over by the lion. There was no fear of the lion even though he looked fierce, no one was shy in drawing close. I found it strange that something so dangerous could be played with like a pet but at the same time there was something about the lion that made you unaware of the danger of being close to such a powerful animal. As I watched the lion, admiring his beauty and wondering what he was doing here, I too began to be almost entranced by him. I forgot where I was and what I had come here for. All I could think about was this amazing lion. His coat was so fine and the mane on his head made him look fierce and attractive.

By now, the attention of nearly everyone in the room had been drawn to the lion. Some people carried on talking to each other but no one was really interested in what their friends had to say anymore. Everyone wanted to be close to the lion. There was even a hint of jealousy in the air when someone seemed to get attention from the lion. The lion turned his head and he looked around the room. As he did so I caught a glint of something in his eye. It looked to me like pride, slowly an unease came over me and a sickening feeling started to turn in my stomach. Who is this lion? I wondered. What is he doing here, what does he want? Even with an unease rising in me about the lion I was still completely enraptured with him.

As the lion looked around, I found myself hoping he would look at me, please come to me next, I thought. As if hearing my thoughts the lion turned his head my way and stared straight into my eyes. I found myself staring back into the eyes of the lion. At first a sense of deep satisfaction went through me, "He's looking at me!" I said to myself feeling a sense of achievement and happiness. The lion held my gaze for what felt like a very long time. As I stared back into the lion's eyes I was suddenly aware of something hidden somewhere deep within the lion. I stared deeper. It was as if I could see past the beautiful coat and into the hidden part of the lion's spirit. At first I couldn't work out what it was, but I grew more and more intrigued about what was within this beautiful beast.

Suddenly I had a revelation from God. It was like I was coming out of a dream to an awakened state. I saw that this great beast was not what he seemed; I saw that there was a darkness in his spirit. Instantly I realised that the lion was not good as I had first thought but that he was full of evil intent. At that moment the lion, knowing my thoughts began to run at me. He ran right into me and knocked me to the floor. His powerful paws swung immediately for my head, just missing my face. I knew he was trying to take out my eyes, to blind me to the truth and prevent me from seeing who he truly was. He was desperate to prevent me from revealing his true nature to the group. The once peaceful lion was now full of fear and rage. The lion leapt forward again and swiped his paw at my face, leaving deep gashes on my head and cheek. I was under the lion trying to use my arms to protect my face as the lion swung his claws at me once again. He hit my arms but was unable to get to my eyes. Someone's arms grabbed me under my shoulders and pulled me out from under the lion. The same arms picked me up and carried me away from the lion's attack, out of the room and into the main hall of our church. I had no idea who had picked me up and saved me from the lion. A few of my friends fled the room behind me but most people stayed in the room, they seemed completely unaware of what had just happened. I was in a daze, my heart was pounding and my mind was so confused, desperately trying to understand what had just happened.

In the hall the young people were playing sports and paid no attention to the blood running all over my head from the deep wounds inflicted on my face by the lion. They seemed oblivious to the worried faces of those who had come out of the room behind me. It wasn't long before a few people who had witnessed the attack in the other room came out to see me. I assumed they were coming to make sure I was *ok but they didn't even seem to care about my well-being, instead of dressing my wounds and helping me overcome the trauma of the attack they began to verbally attack me, defending and rationalising the lion's actions. They said that I must have done something terrible to upset him so much and to make him to behave in such a way. They told me that he was a good lion and that I should move on, get over what happened and not to make a fuss about it.*

————

I woke from my dream feeling shocked. I knew instinctively that the dream I just had was from God. But what did it mean?

We have an Enemy
This dream left me feeling heavy hearted and concerned, with many questions to answer. What was God saying to me? What is this lion? Why didn't anyone realise we were in danger? Are our young people being misled by an evil spirit? Over the next few days as I thought and prayed about the dream, God began to reveal to me its meaning.

It wasn't hard to realise that the lion in my dream represented the devil, his schemes and his demonic strongholds. The apostle Peter wrote in *1 Peter (5:8)*

"Be sober-minded; be watchful.
Your adversary the devil prowls around like a
roaring lion, seeking someone to devour."

And the Apostle Paul taught us in *2 Corinthians*
(11:14)

"And no wonder, for even Satan
disguises himself as an angel of light."

I began to realise that God was showing me one of the devil's strategies to seduce God's people. We are often on guard against sin that is blatant and clear but our enemy, whilst a wild destroyer, presents himself as an angel of light. Often his schemes are subtle and deceiving. Christians are very good at recognising the blatant works of evil in the world but we can miss, or even worse, justify the subtle works of the evil one.

There is a danger that we blame the devil or demons for everything that goes wrong in our lives, but we need to guard our hearts against being superstitious and fearful. However, there is an even greater danger that we ignore the power of the evil one. We are not to fear the devil but neither are we to be ignorant to his schemes.

Some time ago I met with a lady that had started coming to our church. She was searching for truth and God was beginning to move in her life. As we talked she asked why I talked about 'our enemy' so much. "Aren't we supposed to love our enemy?" She asked. I explained to her that when Jesus taught us to love our enemy, he was referring to mankind, not the devil and his demons. As we talked more, I discovered that she felt it was unnecessary to teach about sin and having an enemy. I explained to her that we teach what Jesus taught and he taught us that we have an enemy, that the giving of his life was so that sin could be overcome. I was a little surprised by this lady's thoughts but over the years I have met more and more Christians that don't want to talk about evil spirits, the devil or sin. It is as if these concepts have been resigned to the history books as 'folk tales' and we as an enlightened people know they are not really there. It's sad when people claiming to be 'Christians' choose to exult their own thinking or the opinions of the day above the teachings of Jesus.

As a preacher in the church, I don't often teach on the devil because I don't want to have an over emphasis on his power and authority in the world. However, I want to highlight and teach what Jesus thought and so I am compelled at times to teach about our enemy, his schemes and his workers. When doing so we need to remember that we are not focusing on how great our enemy is but on how great our God is.

Interestingly sometimes people get annoyed when it is suggested that a consistent compelling sin, mindset or a sickness of body or mind could be due to demonic influence. I wonder if that annoyance itself may be something spiritual being provoked. It is possible to accept the demonic realms that influence our lives rather than taking hold of the authority that God has given us to overcome it in the name of Jesus. If we are to be followers of Jesus then we must examine what Jesus taught. Jesus taught us all we need to know about the devil and his schemes.

In *Matthew (13:19)*, Jesus is explaining the parable of the Sower. He tells his disciples:

> *"When anyone hears the word of the*
> *kingdom and does not understand it,*
> *the evil one comes and snatches away*
> *what has been sown in his heart."*

There is a lot of truth here in this parable for us to grasp. One way the devil prevents people from receiving the word of God is through their lack of understanding. Jesus is highlighting a very important principle. The devil is able to snatch away the seed because the hearer hasn't understood. How often we can hear the word of God but then not see the fruit of that word produced in our lives because we don't understand? We can turn this around to see that understanding the word of God is a crucial tool to prevent the enemy stealing away the potential of God's word in our lives. The Gospel and the teachings of scripture are the way of life and the words of God are all that we need for life and godliness. God in His goodness actually gives the gift of teaching to his church, in order to equip His people to rightly apply the teachings of scripture. In 2 Corinthians (4:3-4) Paul writes:

> *"And even if our gospel is veiled,*
> *it is veiled to those who are perishing.*
> *In their case the god of this world has*
> *blinded the minds of the unbelievers,*
> *to keep them from seeing the light*
> *of the gospel of the glory of Christ,*
> *who is the image of God."*

We see here the same principle that Jesus taught His followers through the parable of the Sower. The god of this world, the devil, blinds the eyes of unbelievers so that they cannot see the light of Christ.

There is no doubt when we look in scripture that we have an adversary who wishes to kill, steal and destroy. While we are not to live in fear of our enemy it is a grave mistake to ignore the fact of his existence and his desire to stand against God's church. He does this firstly by seeking to exploit peoples lack of understanding and secondly by blinding or darkening the minds of people to the truth. Our enemy's desire is to kill, steal and destroy what God is seeking to do in His people and on the earth. In *Isaiah (5:13)* God warns his people:

> *"Therefore my people go into exile for lack of knowledge; their honoured men go hungry, and their multitude is parched with thirst."*

Here in Isaiah, it is God's own people Israel that are being destroyed due to their lack of knowledge. They are taken into exile, away from the land that God wanted them to live in under his protection and provision. Not understanding or the lack of knowledge among mankind is an opportunity for the devil to distort and steal what God desires to do in the hearts of mankind. In the parable of the Sower, the seed that was sown had the ability to bring forth a great harvest. Note that in much of the soil it multiplied many times over. The problem is never with the seed, the problem is with the soil. The word of God is able to bring forth a great spiritual harvest in our lives. The enemy's ability to stop that harvest is actually in the individuals' inability or refusal to accept or understand the message of the kingdom. The enemy has no alternative truth, his only power is in making us doubt God. When we believe God that is faith. When we doubt God that is when the enemy is able to steal the seed away.

I realised that through my dream, God was trying to open my eyes to a weakness in our young people at the time. He wanted to warn me of the danger we were in. I also began to see that while the meaning of the dream had an immediate application it also had a wider application for all of God's church.

The immediate meaning
At first, I found it hard to understand how our young people could have been under the influence of the enemy's strategy. From the outward appearance our youth group were a great and spiritual bunch, we were the good ones, we didn't swear, drink, do drugs or get into sexual relationships. We were clean living. Unlike other waves of youth before us who had had a reputation for being rebels, we were 'The Nice Group.' It wasn't fake, we really were well behaved, we had a heart for God and for his church. We served, we witnessed, we cared for each other. We moved in spiritual gifts. God was showing me that something was wrong, but what was it?

As I was meditating on my dream It hit me suddenly. Pride! We were proud. As I thought about it, I began to recognise it more and more. There was an arrogance among us. It wasn't blatant and open but subtle. We had become focused on how great we were, how we were not like other young people. We had begun to trust in our own righteousness and see our success as something we had done ourselves rather than recognising our dependence on God's grace. Pride can be such a subtle sin, it can creep in slowly and craftily. And it has great power to bring destruction. Matthew Henry once said "It was pride that took Lucifer from the throne room of God and it is pride that will keep us from that same throne room." I realised that pride was taking our attention from Jesus and on to ourselves, allowing the enemy to take our attention.

In *James (4:6-10)*, James tells us:

> *"But he gives more grace. Therefore it says,*
> *"God opposes the proud but gives grace to the*
> *humble." Submit yourselves therefore to God.*
> *Resist the devil, and he will flee from you.*
> *Draw near to God, and he will draw near to you.*
> *Cleanse your hands, you sinners, and purify*
> *your hearts, you double-minded. Be wretched*
> *and mourn and weep. Let your laughter be turned*
> *to mourning and your joy to gloom. Humble*
> *yourselves before the Lord, and he will exalt you."*

God was warning me of this subtle yet destructive sin of pride because pride is offensive to him. He opposes the proud but to the humble He will show His grace.
Proverbs (11:2) says:

"When pride comes, then comes disgrace,
but with the humble is wisdom."

Pride in essence is taking for ourselves the honour that is actually due to God. It comes when we begin to think that we have done great things in our own strength, rather than recognising our dependency on God and that this is the work of the Holy Spirit.

God began to remind me of conversations in which we openly said we doubted that there was a better Christian youth group in London.
Was that so bad? We were just young and excited about what we had!
Yes. It was so bad, because it came out of a prideful heart, pride causes me to forsake my need and dependency on God. Pride is a tool that the devil will use to make us ineffective in God's kingdom. It is worth noting that the snake in the garden of Eden said to Eve that if she ate the fruit the tree she and Adam would be like God (*Genesis 3*). He was seeking to cause her to be proud, to esteem herself above God. Pride is when we don't recognise the goodness and greatness of God but rather begin to believe that we are able in our own strength to do the things that only God can do. What was so interesting was that our pride was in how godly we were. Just like the Pharisees in the gospels, the very people that should love and wel-

come Jesus, the people that call themselves God's own are often the very people that due to pride, end up standing against God. We see this highlighted for us in the Gospels where the Pharisees, who should have been the ones to recognise Jesus as the Messiah ended up being the ones that sought His death.

We weren't so bad that we had begun to stand against God and I didn't feel that God was blasting me for being proud, but he was warning me of the path we were on, revealing to me how our attention was being taken away from him. The lion's scheme was to distract us by taking our focus from God and on caring for one another and putting it on what we had achieved and how great we were. We looked at what we had and thought we had made it, that we were so great and our hearts were slowly becoming colder toward God. We were becoming like the Pharisees, more concerned about the outer appearance of things than the state of our own hearts.

In *Romans (2:4)* Paul says:

> *"...not knowing that God's kindness*
> *is meant to lead you to repentance?"*

God in his kindness reveals our sins and weaknesses because he desires us to be free from their power over us. He shows us that we are on the wrong path and leads us to the place of repentance. Because he loves us. His kindness means that if we will listen, He will always warn us and help us to return to His paths.

Repentance means to change the mind or turn around. We were heading in the wrong direction so God showed us what was happening in order that we could see the dangers and turn around. It amazes me that so often when God reveals our weaknesses to us, that instead of repenting we try to justify ourselves. This was represented to me in the dream by my friends telling me it was my fault that the lion got upset. Rather than turning away from loving his attention they were defending him.

As I said, I didn't feel that God was scolding me or our youth group but rather that He was seeking to warn me. He wanted me to see what He saw, to understand that we were allowing our enemy to get in among us through pride. God in His love and grace wanted to wake us up and help us to deal with subtle sins that were creeping in among us. In the natural it may seem a trivial thing for a group of passionate young Christians to have a little pride in themselves! However when we realise that pride is offensive to God and is a foothold for our enemy to begin to draw us away from him, then we should stop at nothing to destroy pride.

This pride came among us as a work of the tempter, about which Jesus warned His disciples when they requested that He teach them to pray. Part of that prayer he taught them, found in *Matthew "6:13"* says:

"And lead us not into temptation,
but deliver us from evil (or the evil one)"

Jesus was telling His disciples that they should pray that they would be delivered from evil. Why? Because evil would try to snare them. God's desire for us is that we should be saved from the schemes and snares of the evil one. This was important enough for him that he made sure it would be part of the believer's prayer.

Through this dream, God was showing me that our young people were making an idol out of our own righteousness. We thought it was a beautiful thing, but actually it was a dangerous beast. We were allowing sin in our lives, it wasn't the blatant sin that is easy to recognise but subtle attitudes and behaviours that led us away from the love of Christ. I was able to share this dream with my friends in the youth and we prayed together, re-committing our hearts to God, we confessed our sin in becoming proud and God continued to do a great work among us.

This lesson has served me well through the years. There have been many times when God has spoken to me about wrong attitudes and thought patterns that have started to become normal to me. I have learned that when I feel a prompting, which often feels like a churning in my stomach. I stop and think whether I have just said or thought something that is not honouring to God. Time and again the Holy Spirit puts His finger on the issue and I am able to repent and get my mind back where it belongs. God loves us and wants us to be like his son in all that we do. He wants us free of the thoughts, fears and lies of the evil one. God wants without exception to deliver us from the evil one and his influences.

Let's Talk About Sin!
It can often be so easy to see sin and failings in the lives of others but we can often be ignorant to its control in our own lives. Sin, no matter how much it appeals to us or how much we justify it, is offensive to God. Sin separated Adam from the presence of God in the garden of Eden. Sin cost Christ his life. Jesus had to endure the cross to overcome the power that sin had over mankind. He was tortured and crucified to reconcile us to God. We must take sin seriously. I have highlighted pride as I believe it was the issue that God was revealing to me in my dream but there are many areas of subtle sin that can creep into a Christians life. For example we can become judgmental, cynical, self-righteous or gossips. Not all sin is obvious, but all

sin is offensive to God and causes us to miss out on the blessings and rewards that God desires to poor out on our lives. As followers of Jesus, we are to set our hearts on becoming more and more like him. This means that throughout our lives we are to seek greater and greater refining. As I will explain this doesn't have to be a dreary lifestyle of self-loathing but rather a joyful discovery of what it means to be holy.

We don't need to live in constant fear that we may have done something offensive to God, but we should be open hearted before God, willing to be challenged and corrected. When we are challenged or convicted then let's determine to change. It's important that we draw a distinction at this point between conviction and condemnation. If reading this chapter so far has caused you to feel challenged and left you with a desire to press on and challenge any areas of sin you are aware of in your life then you are probably feeling convicted. That is a great thing, it means that God is drawing you into holiness by highlighting areas he wants to refine in your life. However, if reading this chapter has caused you to feel ashamed and anxious, then you are probably experiencing a sense of condemnation. Maybe there is even a voice in your head saying "you will never be holy". That is the work of our enemy. He brings condemnation. If you are feeling condemned then I want to tell you right now you are loved by your heavenly Father and He is committed to transforming you in to the image of His Son, Jesus Christ. Don't believe the voice but rather, thank God that He will lead you into freedom and holiness.

Understanding Repentance

God wants His people to embrace repentance. This may sound strange, but true repentance is a joy. It sounds strange because repentance is often associated with weeping and sorrow, and rightly so. There is a place for weeping and godly sorrow but those themselves are not repentance. I have seen lots of people weeping at the alter over their sin but when they get up and go home, nothing changes. They were truly moved by conviction and were grieving over their sin but they didn't repent. I have done the same thing myself many times. I have been confronted with my sin; wept over how it grieves God's heart, promising to change and then the next day committed the same sin again. I'm not saying that our sin shouldn't grieve us but feeling the weight of our sin is not repentance. Repentance is when we leave the old way and walk in a new way, leaving our sin at the foot of the cross and living free of it. We often confuse grief with true repentance. Grief can lead to repentance and it can be the evidence of repentance but if we don't turn away from our sin then it makes no difference how sorry we are or how much we grieve. We have not repented until we turn around and walk in the opposite direction. Turning from sin should produce joy in our hearts. At times when God has revealed sin in my life, I have wept because I have offended the one I love. That weeping is not repentance itself. It is a recognition of my sin and of my need for forgiveness. Repentance is what happens next. It is the walking away from sin and living free of the power that sin had in my life. True repentance brings joy to God's heart and likewise it leads us from captivity to joyous freedom in Christ. So the outworking of repentance in our lives is actually joy that comes because I am free. *Acts (3:19)* says:

> *"Repent therefore, and turn back,*
> *that your sins may be blotted out,*
> *that times of refreshing may come*
> *from the presence of the Lord",*

This realisation struck me one day while I was on a bus in Buenos Aires, Argentina. I had been traveling with some friends around the world on an 8 months trip. We had been in India, South East Asia, Australasia and we had now arrived in South America. By this point in our journey around the world we were all running very low on funds, the three of us ended up staying in a two-man tent for one month. Initially we had planned to travel all over Argentina but with very little money left we ended up staying in a campsite on the outskirts of Buenos Aires and traveling into the city each day by bus to explore the sites.

One day as I rode the bus I was praying and worshiping God. I asked God if there was anything in my life that was not honouring to Him. Suddenly I heard God challenge an attitude in my heart that I had not paid much attention to before. I felt the Holy Spirit say to me "That attitude is ungodly and displeasing to me." I understood immediately why, and I recognised how it had taken hold of my thinking. I remember clearly bowing my head and simply confessing to God that I had sinned by embracing this wrong attitude, I thanked God for revealing it to me and I immediately stopped thinking that way. I repented! What was surprising to me was that all of this took place in just a few moments and during the whole process all I was aware of was God's love and kindness toward me. I felt a joy through the whole process. Repentance had never been like this to me before that day but since then I have had a number of occasions where God has touched my heart in this way and it has been a joy for me to repent. There have also been times since where I have wept with sadness at what my sin had done to others and how it had offended my loving heavenly Father. But the lesson I have learned very clearly is that changed lives are the fruit of repentance not how many tears we cry.

To summarise, repentance happens when we are made aware that our thoughts, feeling or actions are offensive to God, in response to this awareness we acknowledge this sin and we turn from it and stop doing it.

The effects of sin

Often sin's greatest effect is to isolate us and cause us to feel ashamed. We may feel we can't tell anyone about struggling with sin in our lives. We are scared of what people would think about us if they knew our weaknesses and struggles. I have often prayed with people who are reluctant to share their battle with sin as they believe that I will think badly of them. I can understand this thinking, as a young Christian, I thought much that way myself. My father was a minister in our church and I thought that if people knew about any sin in my life it would bring shame on him and the rest of my family. This fear caused me to hide my sin rather than tackling it head on.

Many Christians do not realise that Christ didn't just die to forgive our sin but to free us from slavery to sin. We can believe that sin is our nature and that we are powerless against its pull on our lives, when in fact Christ's gift to us is his righteousness and we can learn to live in his righteousness free from the overwhelming power of and compulsion to sin.

Another of the devil's tactics is to isolate people, to make them think that they are not welcome or don't fit in with others. If we are struggling with a weakness in our lives, he will try to convince us that we are the only one with this problem and that, if we tell anyone about the struggles we are facing, they will not understand but rather will judge and reject us. The Bible tells us that there is no temptation that is not common to man. We are never alone in the temptations we face. This was made clear to me when as a young man I built up the courage to share with some of my friends, the ongoing struggles I was facing. I was so nervous to share as I thought my friends would be disgusted with me. However, to my surprise after talking to them I discovered that they were facing very similar struggles in their own lives. Instead of judging me we became a great encouragement to one another, and we were able to help each other overcome. If Christians could understand that we are not meant to struggle through life on our own but as *Galatians (6:2)* says:

> *"bear one another's burdens and*
> *thereby fulfil the law of Christ",*

then we would find such freedom and hope in our brothers and sisters. The power or temptation to sin is vastly reduced when it is exposed and confessed. Like a dark room hides many objects, once the curtain is opened and light is let in it is much easier to see what you stumbled over in the dark and to then put things in order.

Our accuser, the devil, tells us we are all alone and that no one will love or forgive us for the wrongs we have done. Maybe our greatest failing is that we are slow to believe the word of God but easily listen to and accept the lies of the enemy. In my teen years and into early adulthood, I saw myself as a sinner and I believed I had to fight for the rest of my life to stop sin from overcoming me. I didn't realise that Christ had already overcome sin for me, all I needed to do was to begin to live in the freedom that He had bought for me.

If you have struggled with sin, you may will find it hard to believe that you can just stop. Could it really be that simple? Well, yes and no. Of course, we have to learn to stand against temptation and there are times we have to wrestle against sinful desires. I am not suggesting that we don't have to apply effort and discipline to overcome sin. However, I found that many Christians are battling sin from an unbiblical stance and need a shift in their understanding. We have been freed from the rule of sin over our lives. It is no longer our master, Christ is! Sin is not our natural way anymore, righteousness is!

No longer a sinners
We must learn to take sin seriously. Not just feeling bad for it but turning away from it. Pride, unforgiveness, anger and bitterness are sin just as murder and adultery are sin, God hates it all. God calls us to repent, turn, walk away from our sinful behaviours and live differently, as we surrender our lives to Him. Paul tells us in *Romans (6:11-13)*

*"So you also must consider yourselves
dead to sin and alive to God in Christ Jesus.
Let not sin therefore reign in your mortal body,
to make you obey its passions. Do not present
your members to sin as instruments for
unrighteousness, but present yourselves to God
as those who have been brought from death to life,
and your members to God as instruments for
righteousness."*

Paul instructs us that we are to consider ourselves dead to sin. That can seem easier said than done! I believe that one of the biggest hindrances for many Christians seeking to overcoming sin in their lives is that they continue to live with the mindset that they are sinners and incapable of overcoming sin. In one way they are right, we can't overcome sin by ourselves. Only Christ could overcome sin. The good news is that He did! And because he did, we can too.

We have been made righteous in Christ. The battle with sin is all but won when we realise we are no longer sinners because of Christ's sacrifice. I am not saying we can't sin, just that it should not be our nature anymore. We are made into a new creation and now rather than 'sin' being our nature, righteousness is now our new nature.

In 2 Corinthians (5:17-21) Paul says:

"Therefore, if anyone is in Christ, he is a new creation. The old has passed away; behold, the new has come. All this is from God, who through Christ reconciled us to himself and gave us the ministry of reconciliation; that is, in Christ, God was reconciling the world to himself, not counting their trespasses against them, and entrusting to us the message of reconciliation. Therefore, we are ambassadors for Christ, God making his appeal through us. We implore you on behalf of Christ, be reconciled to God. For our sake he made him to be sin who knew no sin, so that in him we might become the righteousness of God."

"Become the righteousness of God". Wow! Think about that for a moment. I'm not just forgiven but I have become God's righteousness. In Christ I am a righteous man! That means that my standing is upright, good and acceptable to God. The opposite of sinner. A sinner misses the mark, falls short and isn't acceptable. To be righteous means I hit the mark, reach the level and am totally acceptable to God. I am righteous! You are righteous! Not by works that we have performed but by the mercy of God.

It is important to be aware of the devil's schemes. Our enemy is not stupid, he knows how to mislead us, he's been doing it for thousands of years. The devil's plan is to take our attention away from God and from others around us, he knows that if our eyes are off God we will lose our strength, so he will always work to distract us. He wants us to be focused on unimportant things, to be obsessed by worldly ambitions so that living for God is not the priority in our lives. He brings strife among us so that we are consumed in fighting one another rather than fighting against him.

If we desire to serve God and to live in the righteousness that he has given us, then we must be willing to allow God to reveal sin in in our lives. We must repent, walking away from that sin, consider ourselves dead to that sin and walk into the righteousness that Christ has bought for us. Praise God that He has the last word. He, in His kindness is speaking to us. "Wake up, look into the eyes of what you thought would bring you pleasure and see its true nature. Turn from your sin and live in the freedom bought for you with my blood. You are no longer a slave to sin."

This word slave really sums up our new relationship to sin. Before we received Christ into our hearts, we were slaves to sin. It was our master. Once we receive Christ in our lives, we are no longer slaves to sin, sin can still seek to control us but it is not our master any more, Jesus is. We are no longer obliged to do what sin wants, we are free not slaves.

Overcoming sin

Knowing that Jesus paid the price for our sin and that in Him we are no longer seen by God as sinners but as 'the righteousness of Christ' is a great comfort. But that isn't the end of the matter. We can believe this is true but still struggle with the pull of sinful desire in our lives.

I want to share with you some practical steps to help deal with sin. These are all steps that I have learned in my own walk with Jesus and that have helped me to overcome sin's influence in my own life.

1.Consider yourself dead to sin

Firstly, we need to stop thinking of ourselves as sinners. What I mean by this is stop thinking that you can't help it because it is your nature! No it isn't. As a Christian You are a new creation. Jesus shed his blood not only so you can be forgiven but so that you can be free from the power of sin. In *Romans (6:1-6)*, Paul tells us

"What shall we say then? Are we to continue in sin that grace may abound? By no means! How can we who died to sin still live in it? Do you not know that all of us who have been baptised into Christ Jesus were baptised into his death? We were buried therefore with him by baptism into death, in order that, just as Christ was raised from the dead by the glory of the Father,

we too might walk in newness of life.
For if we have been united with him in a death
like his, we shall certainly be united with him in a
resurrection like his. We know that our old self
was crucified with him in order that the body of
sin might be brought to nothing, so that we
would no longer be enslaved to sin."

Your *"old self was crucified with him".* That means it died. When we come to Christ and are born again, the old self dies and the new self comes to life. We are a new person. That can be hard to get our minds around as we still inhabit the same body, have the same memories and we may still have the same likes and dislikes. If we believe what the bible teaches then we should see ourselves as a new creation. That old me just doesn't exist anymore. Talking to people about their conversion, you often hear the same thing. "I just felt like I was a new person". It's not just a metaphor it's true. The old has gone, the new has come. The old self previously formed many of our characteristics and thought patterns. We have to be tenacious as we allow our new life to be transformed into the image of Christ. Our natural tendency will be to respond as we always did in the past, but we don't have to. We can be very different. We can listen to the Holy Spirit as He brings the word of God alive to us and instructs us in who we are.

Let me tell a story to help us understand this idea better. A fictional man, Lenny, was convicted of murder when he was 18 years old. The story goes like this. One night Lenny and his best friend went out drinking together. Lenny got really drunk and had no memory of what happened to him and his best friend. The next morning Lenny's best friend was found brutally murdered in an alleyway. He had been stabbed many times and left to bleed out. Lenny was found by the police soon after, passed out under a bridge not far from the murder scene. He was covered in his friend's blood and had the knife that was used in his hand. It was clear to everyone that Lenny was guilty. At the trial he was sentenced to life in prison.

Before the murder Lenny had been an average guy but after he murdered his best friend, everything changed. His identity was now that of a murderer. He lived with constant guilt and shame for what he had done. In prison Lenny had to learn to protect himself and became violent and angry. He hated himself for what he had done. He hated the guards for the way they judged him. He hated the other inmates. He always had to protect himself, he couldn't show any weakness.

Now, an old man that had lived near the sight of the murder had witnessed what happened that night but had died the next morning after the horrific event. We will call the old man Burt. Burt had been wheelchair bound and had been unable to leave his bed to tell anyone what he had seen that night. Burt though was a great writer and he had written in his journal what he had seen. The old man's daughter inherited the house and had packed up the journals and put them in the loft for safe keeping. Many years later Burt's granddaughter had been clearing up the loft and came across the old diaries. As she sat for hours reading through them, she finally came to the last entry. It told the account of the last night of her grandfather's life and what he had seen through the window that night.

Burt told in his journal how he had seen two young men going into the alleyway and that another young man had followed them and held them up at knife point. One of the young men had stepped forward to protect his friend who could hardly stand. The attacker then stabbed the brave young man several times dropped the knife and ran. The second young man collapsed in a heap on the floor over his companion. After some hours the second young man picked up the knife and staggered away. Burt's granddaughter immediately called the police and informed them what she had found.

Within a short time Lenny was free from prison. He was given a large sum of money as compensation for the wrongful imprisonment. Lenny returned to his family. He was so happy to be home and to be free but his years of seeing himself as a murderer, thinking like a murderer being treated like a murderer made it very difficult for him to adjust to a life outside prison after being set free.

Do you get the picture? Lenny was conditioned to act and think a particular way due to his perceived identity as a murderer. When his identity changed, when he was told he was no longer a guilty man but an innocent man, his nature and behaviour didn't change all at once.

Many Christians are like Lenny. They have lived with the weight of feeling guilty of sin. Even when they accept that Jesus has paid the price for their sin and set them free, they still live as if they are still a sinner. The problem for Lenny was that prison was all he had come to know, he had to re-condition his thinking and so do we. Our bent toward sin is no longer because sin is our nature but because it 'was' our nature and we have to learn to live in the 'new' nature, that is available to us in Christ.

The first step to winning our battle with sin is to stop thinking that we can't help it and to realise that in Christ we are now dead to sin!

2. You can always say no
I remember my Dad telling me as a little boy that we always have a choice to do what is right or wrong. We have a choice because Jesus set us free

from being a slave to sin. Yes, we can still sin but we are now free to say no. No matter how compelled we feel to do something we always have a choice. I remember times as a young man, battling the desire to do something I knew was wrong. I have been at the point where I had been physically shaking, fighting against ungodly desire. Jesus went through something far greater than this in the garden of Gethsemane.

We find the account in *Luke (22:44):*

> *"And being in agony he prayed more earnestly;*
> *and his sweat became like great drops*
> *of blood falling down to the ground".*

Jesus was in such turmoil in the garden as He chose to submit to God's will of enduring the cross, that He sweat blood. The temptation to sin can be overwhelming but we can always say no because sin is not our master. Saying no to sin is saying yes to honouring our Lord. Our struggle is not the same as unbelievers. We have the Holy Spirit that empowers us in our weakness. We can build spiritual character and we can call on the Holy Spirit for strength in times of temptation.

There are times where desires, anger or jealousy can feel overwhelming, in these times our character and resolve are tested, and it can feel like we just can't overcome but take comfort in God's promise that he will not allow you to be tempted beyond what you can stand. *1 Corinthians (10:13)* tells us:

> *"No temptation has overtaken you that is not common to man. God is faithful, and he will not let you be tempted beyond your ability, but with the temptation he will also provide the way of escape, that you may be able to endure it."*

So when you are   facing temptation, know that God will provide a way out, an exit door. Keep saying no and ask God where the exit is.

3. Change your desires

Realising that God can help my desires to change was a massive breakthrough for me. *James (1:13-15)* tells us:

> *"Let no one say when he is tempted,*
> *"I am being tempted by God," for God cannot be tempted with evil, and he himself tempts no one. But each person is tempted when he is lured and enticed by his own desire. Then desire when it has conceived gives birth to sin, and sin when it is fully grown brings forth death."*

From this passage it is important to note that God is not the one tempting us. It is our desires that are the problem. We are led astray because we desire what is wrong. The answer then is that we need to have our desires changed. I have found that through prayer and intimacy with God my desires do change. No longer do I want to go my own way, but I want to do the things that are pleasing to my Lord. We can pray that He will change our desires and like King David we can ask God to renew a right spirit within us (*Psalm 51*).

In *Romans (12:2)* we are told:

> *"Do not be conformed to this world,*
> *but be transformed by the renewal of your mind,*
> *that by testing you may discern what is the will*
> *of God, what is good and acceptable and perfect."*

The renewing of our mind transforms us. God wouldn't give us an instruction to renew our minds if it wasn't possible. It is more than possible; in fact it should be normal Christian experience. As we read God's word, spend time with God in prayer and worship and fellowship with other believers we should expect that our thinking and our desires will change to be more honouring and pleasing to God. If you recognise that there are desires in you that would lead you into sin given the opportunity, then tell God what they are and ask him to change those desires.

I remember reading the above passage of scripture some years ago and feeling like my eyes had been opened by the Holy Spirit to its meaning for the first time. I realised that the problem was that we desired things that are against God's design for our lives. We can ask God to change our desires and allow Him to work in us to cause our desires to come into line with His. I have applied this principle in my life over the years and it has been such a blessing to me. If I become aware that my desires are at odds with God's and potentially could entice me to sin, I will bring this before God in prayer and sometimes will share it with a Christian friend. I ask God to work in me, changing my desires. Over time I begin to see that the thing that would once have been an area of temptation in my life has changed and I no longer desire that thing anymore.

I remember one day talking with a friend that had been an alcoholic and drug addict for many years. He had become a Christian in prison. As we talked, he told me that he was an alcoholic. I was surprised as I had never seen him drunk or any of the signs that he had a problem with alcohol. "When was the last time you had a drink", I asked. "Some years ago", he answered. "Then you're not an alcoholic any more", I said. "Yes I am, I will always be an alcoholic", he replied defensively. We talked a while longer and I came to realise that part of his recovery had been to acknowledge that he was an addict. That is a very important part of recovery and often necessary for people to begin to find freedom from addiction. However, the second point he had had to accept was that he would always be an addict. This is where I believe we have to be careful. It is one thing to acknowledge that we have an addiction but it is another to accept that we will never change. I want to be clear here. I am not saying that people who have had addictions should not be aware of their tendency to return to their addiction. If someone has been an alcoholic, it may be wise that they choose not to drink alcohol again as this could be a stumbling block to them. My concern though, is in accepting the idea that we will never truly be free of our addiction. This mindset denies the power of God to break addiction and change our desires. My friend was choosing to identify himself as an addict even though he was not addicted to drugs or drink at this point in his life. His identity was someone that would forever be addicted, rather than enjoying the fact that he had overcome addiction and recognise that God could change his desires so that he no longer needed to fear addiction. Addiction is a complex struggle, often with root issues in our lives. We need wisdom in dealing with addiction and their roots. Freedom from addiction is not a license to put ourselves back into situations where we can be tempted.

Take Action
If you struggle with an area of temptation or addiction in your life, I encourage you to be honest with about your weakness with godly friends and most importantly with the Holy Spirit. If needed

seek out other believers that can stand with you in prayer. Ask the Holy Spirit to change your desires and to form in you new godly desires.

4. Turn temptation to praise

I have discovered that turning temptations to praise is one of the greatest weapons a Christian has at their disposal. This came alive to me when I decided to deal with an area of temptation in my life. Whenever I felt tempted, I would immediately feel ashamed, even as I resisted the temptation. "How is it that I feel like this even when I am not going to do these things" I asked myself. I was making the choice not to give into temptation, but I felt as guilty as if I had been led astray. Then one day something profoundly changed in me. I remember it clearly; I don't know how but my whole mindset shifted. I suddenly felt the grip of temptation on my mind. Immediately I felt a battle inside. Guilt came flooding in, but then I was aware that God was with me. I turned my attention to God and began to thank Him that He had saved me from a life pursuing my sinful desires. "Thank you, God, that you rescued me from sin, that I am yours and yours alone. Thank you that I have turned away from a life that displeases you, that you have rescued me". As I prayed this prayer I could feel the shame falling away. Similar scenarios were repeated again and again over the next several months. After some time I began to notice that I was no longer overcome by feelings of guilt, what had been temptations to me in the past now felt like a reminder of God's goodness in my life. I was able to praise God through the temptation and the temptation lost its power as my desires changed and I no longer accepted the feelings of guilt and shame. I no longer desired the things that once enticed me. Christ has forgiven me, given me his righteousness and now changed the very desires that used to entice my heart as I have allowed the Holy Spirit to work in me.

In *2 Corinthians (10:3-4)* we read:

> *"For though we walk in the flesh, we are not*
> *waging war according to the flesh. For the*
> *weapons of our warfare are not of the flesh*
> *but have divine power to destroy strongholds.*
> *We destroy arguments and every lofty opinion*
> *raised against the knowledge of God, and take*
> *every thought captive to obey Christ,"*

That's what we are doing when we turn temptation to praise; we are "*take*(ing) *every thought captive to obey Christ"*. We don't allow our thought life to control us but rather we control our thought life. This same principle works in many ways. When you are anxious about your needs, turn the anxious thoughts to a prayer for God's provision. When you are angry, turn your anger to a prayer for God to reveal truth to you and to those that you are angry with so that you can be restored to right relationship in love. Take the thought captive before it captures you!

5. Get accountable

When we are struggling with sin in our lives the last thing we want to do is share our weaknesses with others. Secrecy though, is sin's greatest friend. *James (5:16)says:*

"Therefore, confess your sins to one another and pray for one another, that you may be healed."

I know this verse is about healing, but overcoming sin is a type of healing. Confession enables things to be put right in our lives.

How do you clean your home? I have to admit housework isn't my favourite pastime. When we have guests coming to our home we will look for any little hole to hide the things that have been left lying around. We want to give the impression that our home is tidy and in order. However, in reality the cupboards are about to burst open with all the junk we hid in them just before our guests arrived. This is a great illustration of how we can be spiritually. We clean and polish the outside and wear devotion to God like a beautiful robe, however under our robe, our flesh is diseased and we are covered in scars. Does it matter? No one sees these things! Yes, it matters more than we could imagine. God is concerned who we are when no one sees. Who is the true me? The one the world sees or the me that I am on my own with no one around? Both are aspects of me but who I am when only God sees is the one that matters the most. I should do what is right for the love of God and for holiness's sake, not because people are watching. I must say no to sin because I am not a sinner and I don't want to grieve the heart of the one I love, not because I want to look good in public. Letting people in by sharing our weakness is a great way to overcome the power of sin. I chose many years ago to make myself vulnerable and to be accountable to a group of friends. This accountability enabled me to overcome much of the temptation I was facing and in turn I was able to be a help to my friends that were facing similar battles. Sharing our struggles is like bringing light into dark places and often just sharing greatly reduces the burden we are carrying.

Being open and vulnerable is not easy and some people have used my openness against me. I know though, that for many my willingness to be transparent and open with my failings has made it possible for them to find hope and healing.

Dealing with sin in our lives can be a real battle so seeing ourselves as God's righteousness and knowing we are not slaves will make a great impact on our lives but there will still be times of battle to overcome our old nature. When we decide to take back ground that our enemy has occupied in our lives we can find that we enter a time of spiritual battle.

When as a young man I made the decision that I would deal with areas of sin in my own life, I entered a time of real spiritual battle. God was so gracious to me though, He warned me that things were going to get hard. I was attending a bible camp and a well-known Christian leader called people who felt they had a call to prophetic ministry to come forward. I stood in a long line of people and the leader came along the line laying hands on each person as he reached them. Many fell down under the weight of the presence of God. The leader came to me. He didn't lay his hand on me or even pray for me. He looked me in the eyes and said, "God says you have been going through a very difficult battle and that it is going to get worse". After saying this he moved on. I was totally overwhelmed, I fell on the floor and wept.

Normally I would not accept a prophetic word like that as it could have the effect of demoralising the hearer. We have to be very careful when sharing words from God that they don't bring unintentional effects on the hearer. However, on this occasion I knew it was true and rather than it being condemning it was greatly encouraging. You see if the battle had got harder without this word I would have questioned if it would ever end? I would have wondered if there was any hope. Because God had told me it would get harder, I wasn't overwhelmed when it did.

If we don't face the issues of temptation and sin in our lives then we will be hindered from living in the fullness of what God has given us in this life. We can't deal with these issues in our own strength, we need the power of the Holy Spirit to bring change and we need brothers and sisters to walk through our trials with us.

God shows us the mistakes and failures of the mighty men and women in the Bible, so that we can learn from their mistakes and so that we can see that no one   but Jesus was without sin. It is time for God's people to stop hiding their sins and start exposing them, repenting and living free. For only when darkness is exposed to light will it be overcome. Vulnerability, honesty, confession and accountability are the keys to freedom from sin in the Christians life. Pride, secrecy, suspicion and isolation will only keep us in bondage.

Will facing your sin bring you greater trial? Maybe, maybe not! But if it does then be encouraged that you have made the demonic opposition against you uncomfortable and that the one that began a good work in you, will bring it to completion.

6. Break the strongholds
Another area we must consider is that often sin is an invitation to demonic powers to come and have influence over our lives. When we find ourselves

compelled to do what we don't want to do, then we need to consider that there could be another force involved. Jesus in His ministry spent much time freeing people from the power of evil spirits and He commissioned the disciples to do the same. Unfortunately, deliverance sometimes gets a bad press as people seek by human ability to drive out spirits or mix Christian teaching with elements of other false religions, but just because something is given a bad name by frauds and the overzealous, doesn't mean that we should abandon a clearly biblical practice. We must recognise the importance of breaking the strongholds that may have formed over our lives. I thank God that I was brought up in a church that taught and practiced deliverance with wisdom and integrity. This ministry has brought freedom into many people's lives.

Ephesians (6:12) makes this point very clearly:

> *"For we do not wrestle against flesh and blood, but against the rulers, against the authorities, against the cosmic powers over this present darkness, against the spiritual forces of evil in the heavenly places."*

"We don't wrestle against flesh and blood," Note we do 'wrestle' but our wrestling is not in the natural but in the spiritual realm. *"...against the rulers, against the authorities, against the cosmic powers over this present darkness."* I don't think it can be

put much clearer. We will have and we do have a battle on our hands against evil forces that will seek to pin us down and control us. How do they do this? Well one way is by enticing us to sin and then keeping us captive to that sin. Their weapon is the very thing that Jesus has set us free from and they no longer have a position of authority over us beyond what we give them. If you find that you are compelled to sin or tormented with ungodly thoughts, be open to the possibility that you may need deliverance. Seek out a reputable church that practices deliverance and ask for ministry. You can always get a friend to pray with you. Tell whatever has been hounding you to leave in the name of Jesus and invite the Holy Spirit to come and abide in you. You may need to persevere but remember that God desires your complete freedom and He promises that He will complete the good work He begins in us.

7. Redraw the boundaries
One other lesson we can learn, is to redraw our boundary lines. Or to put it another way define our boundaries. We have to be responsible for setting in place a protection around us that will stop us from being drawn into sin. For example, if you are someone that struggles with drinking too much alcohol and you have been convicted of this but keep going too far, ask the Holy Spirit to help you set a boundary. Ask him what your limit should be. Maybe he will tell you stop drinking alcohol for a time. Let him lead you and show you

what is necessary for you. If you find that you get drawn into gossip and can't seem to stop, ask the Holy Spirit to help you set a line that you shouldn't cross. Don't make it right near the edge, where you could easily go too far but set it some distance back so that if you cross it there is no danger of you falling into sin. This doesn't work as a rule book, but it works when we ask God, by His Holy Spirit, to show us what our boundaries should be. The Holy Spirit knows us better than we will ever know ourselves and He is the best judge of what our boundaries should be. It won't be the same for everyone. I have never had a problem with drinking alcohol. I have never been drunk and to be honest I have no desire to drink so for me I have a freedom in this area. I can take it or leave it and I don't need to think about not going too far. However when it comes to what I watch, I have found that I have to be careful as some programmes sow thoughts in my mind that are unhelpful to me. So, my boundaries need to be much clearer and better established in this area. This is a very simple but powerful way of bringing God into our daily lives.

8. Walk in the Spirit
We've saved the most important till last. *Galatians (5:16-17) tells us:*

> *"But I say, walk by the Spirit, and you will not gratify the desires of the flesh. For the desires of the flesh are against the Spirit, and the desires*

*of the Spirit are against the flesh, for these
are opposed to each other, to keep you
from doing the things you want to do."*

The followers of Jesus are so blessed that they
have the Holy Spirit in them and with them at all
times. He can empower us to live holy lives. When
we are in the place of temptation, He is there to
strengthen us. Sometimes the simplest answers
are the most profound. The Holy Spirit is God with
us in the middle of all our trials and temptations.
Simply but powerfully God has made Himself
available to us, His own presence in us can shatter
the power of sin. Nothing can stand against the
Holy Spirit. No demonic power can force you into
sin when the Holy Spirit is your strength. Speaking
of the Holy Spirit, Jesus said that we should come
to Him and drink and out of us will flow rivers of
living water. Ask Jesus to fill you with the Holy
Spirit. Ask the Spirit to lead you, help you and
purify you. He will respond to you. Jesus promised
that the Spirit will be our counsellor. This idea of
walking in the Spirit means that we are in regular
communion with Him. We are to be led by him, as
we listen to his voice.

Every Christian enters salvation through the work
of the Holy Spirit, having begun in the Spirit we
must guard against the temptation to continue on
in our own strength. It is the abiding presence of
the Holy Spirit in our lives that causes us to love

more truly, live more righteously and serve more faithfully. There is so much more that could be said about walking with the Holy Spirit but I am going to explore this in greater depth in a later chapter.

Take Action
Returning to the dream. The lion showed no aggression, he didn't attack anyone as long as everyone was paying attention to him, he only attacked me when I saw the truth. One of the devil's tactics is to keep us from knowing the truth, he wants to blind us. There are two ways we can be kept from seeing truth, the first is to be blinded, the other is to be distracted. *Isaiah (42:6-7)* tells us that Jesus was to come and open the eyes of the blind. Outside of Christ we were spiritually blind and unable to see the truth. We needed a revelation of Jesus to receive our spiritual sight. Once we were born again it was as if we begin to see for the first time. Our spiritual eyes were opened. Now we can see, we need to learn to not be distracted but continue to look and perceive with our spiritual eyes. The devil is the deceiver. If he can't keep us blind then he will seek to keep us deceived and distracted.

Let me explain; As a follower of Jesus, I now know that I have a loving father who has sent His spirit to live in me, to guide me and teach me his nature. That is the last thing that the devil wants. He no longer has dominion over me, but he will still try to do all he can to stop me living in the fullness of

God. He does this by distractions. He wants to occupy my focus so that I won't look to Jesus. Distractions can take many forms. Like rocks in a river they can stop the straight flow of God's spirit in and through our lives. Here are just a few examples of how the devil seeks to distract us. As you read each one, ask the Holy Spirit to show you if any are having an influence on you. If so, ask the Holy Spirit to help you deal with them, removing them from your life. Ask if there are other distractions that the devil has used in your life that are not mentioned here. As you do so, remember this process is not meant to lead us into shame and regret but into repentance, freedom and hope.

Distractions
1. Doubting or Questioning God
One of the devil's oldest tricks is to get mankind to doubt God. Right back in Genesis we see the serpent sowing a thought in Eve's mind. "Did God really say?". Entertaining this thought was the root of disobedience that led to the great fall of mankind. Faith in its most basic form is believing God and faith is powerful. The devil will do all he can to prevent God's people living in the power of faith. He will always try to get us to question and doubt God. *Numbers (23:19)* tells us that *"God is not a man that He should lie".* God doesn't lie! All He says is true. It amazes me how often Christians don't believe God and don't believe God's written word. The enemy wants us to doubt God. He will use disappointments and doubts to undermine

and question God's word. I have even seen him use people's desire for understanding to cause them to question God's word. Are there promises that God has made to you either through scripture or through a prophetic word that you have ceased to trust in because of the lies of the enemy? If so, ask God to restore faith in your heart.

2. Relationship Issues

The Church in my experience is the most loving community on earth but even in the Church there are arguments, jealousies, rejection, judgments and divisions. The devil loves to cause division among God's people. As a local church we have decided never to be divided over minor issues of doctrine and Christian practice. We have learned to be more concerned with the state of someone's heart than with their position on predestination or their eschatological understanding. Sometimes we have had to say goodbye to people that have walked away from us, sometimes those people have caused us pain and spoken ill of us but we are learning that God is more interested in how we deal with hurt and rejection than he is about us always being right. Over the years I have tried to define some cultural values for myself and my family. One that I have sought to apply, is that it is better to be wronged than to wrong someone else. I am not saying that I always live up to this ideal, but it helps me to not take offence and it helps me to keep right relationship with others even when I feel I have been mistreated. In Romans (5:18) Paul tells us,:

> *'If possible, so far as it depends*
> *on you, live peaceably with all.'*

We are to do all we can to be at peace with all people, especially our Christian brothers and sisters. Has the enemy caused relationship issues in your life? Are there Christian brothers and sisters that you are not in right relationship with? Relationship issues are a massive distraction from seeing what God wants us to see. What do you need to do to put these relationships right?

A young woman once told me in conversation that she hated her father. I stopped her and told her that she didn't hate him, she looked a little cross, "Yes I do" she responded. I was shocked to hear this lovely young Christian woman say such a thing. We took some time to talk things through and discussed what it meant to hate someone. I explained that she had no right to hate someone, especially her father because the bible teaches us that we are to honour our parents. We are not allowed to hate them, it's not an option. After some time, she took back her words, and we were able to pray together for her dad, over a short time her relationship with her father vastly improved. She came to tell me how things had changed between them. God had worked wonders in their relationship because this young woman had been willing to forgive her father. The father hadn't been the one to instigate the change, it was the daughter's willingness to forgive him that had begun the healing process. The young lady also noticed something else, her relationship with God had also begun to flourish.

This change was only possible because she was able to see the truth that she was being misled by the devil's schemes and that by repenting and forgiving her father, God worked to turn things around. The bible teaches us to honour our parents! It doesn't say honour your parents if they are good and don't bother if they are bad. How is that possible? The problem is we don't understand honour and respect. We tend to bestow honour on people because of their achievements but God honours us because of who we are, not what we have done. God has given us the gift of being called his children. This is the highest honour there is. Who earned this honour? None of us. When we are told to honour someone in power it is not because that person has earned our respect but because of who they are. Look at the life of King David and how he honoured King Saul despite how Saul treated him. David didn't honour Saul because he earned it or deserved it but because he understood God's perspective on honour. David saw that there were people in his world that he should honour, that he was to follow the order of things and do right no matter how he was being treated. We should honour leaders because it is the right thing to do, not just because we feel honour has been earned. Recently after speaking about honouring and submitting to governmental authority, someone challenged me. Their point was that our government do ungodly things, how can we honour and obey leaders who are ungodly? This is a good question and one that deserves our consideration.

In response let me draw your attention to what we are told in 1 Peter (2:13-15)

"Be subject for the Lord's sake to every human institution, whether it be to the emperor as supreme, or to governors as sent by him to punish those who do evil and to praise those who do good. For this is the will of God, that by doing good you should put to silence the ignorance of foolish people."

On the face of it Peter's instruction looks reasonable. He is telling the church to be subject to, obey, honour and respect those in positions of governmental authority over us. However, we need to understand the context in which Peter is writing. He is not speaking of an elected government, chosen by a democratic process. He is saying that his readers should submit to and obey the emperor. Who is that? The Roman emperor was a tyrannical dictator whose desire was to bring the whole world under his power and dominion. He was a wicked, unrighteous ruler. However, God instructed his people to honour this man because he was in a position of power. We live in a very different time; we have the ability to protest and vote for who we wish to represent us in government and we should use our rights and stand for what we believe in. At the same time though, making sure we are obeying scripture and that means we honour and obey those in authority over us. I realise that this idea can be misunderstood so let me say clearly: God is our first authority and so if an earthly authority asks us to do something against God's command then the answer should always be, respectfully, "no".

3. Disappointment
Disappointment comes for many different reasons. We may have had expectations that were unmet, being let down by those we looked to for help or believing to see a loved one healed that eventually died of their sickness. Whatever the reason may be, you can be sure that the devil will seek to use it to stop you trusting in God. I remember as a young man joining with many in my church to pray for the healing of a new baby born to a couple in our church. The baby was in intensive care with major complications after birth. We held evening prayer times and fasted. We all longed to see the child healed. A few weeks later I was visiting another part of the country with a mission team from New Zealand. One evening while there,

I received a message that the little baby had passed away. At the time I was in a church service. I quietly left the meeting and walked across the field outside the church. I began to cry, "God why did you let this happen", I asked. Immediately I heard a response, "It's not for you to know why Nathanael. It is for you to seek my hand to move". For many, this answer may seem empty but for me it resolved something in my heart, it was more than just the words, something inside me was changed in that moment. I realised that I was disappointed because I had paid a price, I had fasted, given up my time and cried out to God. In return I had expected God to answer my request, by giving me what I asked for. I was disappointed not because God didn't do what He said he would do but because He didn't do what I wanted and expected Him to do. I believe with all my heart that God is our healer, I believe that He could have healed that little child. In this lifetime I will never know why He didn't. Maybe when I see Him face to face I will ask Him "why?". But probably when I do see Him, the question will become irrelevant. We are called to be people of faith and to pursue God for signs and wonders and miracles. I have learned that I need to be willing to seek them while being OK with not finding them. I want to build an expectation in my life for God to move but I need to always remember, He is God and I can't control Him. I have seen God work miracles many times, but I have also missed out on seeing God move many times because I have given place to disappointment and not continued to pursue healing and God's miraculous intervention.

I am not able to bring about a miracle. All I can do is seek the one who can, to move. I have decided I would rather pray for 50 sick people and see 1 healed than pray for no one and see no one healed. One way to deal with disappointment is to share it. We may feel people will think we are faithless if we confess we have disappointment but all we are really doing is expressing our true thoughts and feelings.

Take Action
Ask yourself:
Have I stopped pursuing breakthrough due to disappointment?
Has my history stopped me pursuing God to move in my life?
If you feel you have become disillusioned, Confess this with someone that will encourage you and pray with you for God to restore your hope and confidence in God.

4. Identity
A wrong understanding of our identity can be a massive issue for many Christians. If we have flaws in our character, then we believe there is nothing we can do about it. Do you struggle with anger? If so, has the devil whispered in your ear that 'it is just your temperament, there is nothing

you can do about it'? Don't believe it, that is a lie. Christ has made you a new creation. You are righteous. In Christ we are a new creation, that means we are no longer to see ourselves as we used to be but rather to recognise that we are who He says we are. You are a child of God, welcomed member of His household. Our enemy will always seek to keep us believing that we are weak, sinful failures who will never be acceptable to God but our Father declares over us that we are the head and not the tail (Deuteronomy 28:13), we are the righteousness of God (2 Corinthians 5:21) and we are more than conquerors (Romans 8:37).

Action Point
If you struggle to see yourself as God sees you, ask the Holy Spirit to reveal to you your true identity in Christ. Ask Him to show you how God sees you.

I have found that when we recognise an area where the enemy's lies have had an influence on our thinking, that it can still be a battle to break that influence. This is because our adversary doesn't want to willingly give up ground but rather wants to keep his influence over us. We can be sure though that as we walk in obedience to Christ and resist the devil, he will flee away from us (*James 4:7*). We can always empower to overcome. The key is to obey, live holy lives in obedience to Christ's lordship, and resist; stand firm against opposition and temptation. As James says here, *"he* (the devil) *will flee from you"*! Note that

James doesn't say he might but that "he will". I started by saying I don't like giving credit to the devil, he is not an equal opposite to God. In fact, he is nothing before the power and authority of our God. God has ordained that as we continue to submit to him and resist our enemy then he will flee. He won't walk away slowly but run away in terror as he encounters Christ in us. Let's not be naive to the fact that we have an enemy but let's also not be afraid of our enemy who runs in terror at the presence of our Lord and Saviour Jesus Christ.

In my dream I was helped by unseen hands that took me out of harm's way and placed me in a safe place. God is on our side and no matter how strong our enemy may seem he is only a fallen angel. God is the one and only, true, living God. There is no contest. They are not equally matched opponents; one is the all powerful creator and the other a limited created being.

Our Response to those attacked by the enemy
We need to be careful about how we react to people who have been attacked by the enemy. When we should be encouragers of the distressed, rather too often we pour blame and condemnation on them. I remember once going as a teenager to see a church leader for prayer regarding an area of struggle in my life. The leader told me how awful this thing was and that he had no sympathy for my sin. I felt so humiliated, not because I didn't

agree with his stance on sin, but because there was no grace and encouragement for the one seeking to overcome sin. I didn't want him to sympathise with my sin, I wanted him to sympathise with me for how this sin had caused me to be in bondage. I needed to be encouraged, I needed the leader to recognise that it had taken courage to open up and share my weakness. I needed to know that God loved me and that he would help me to be restored. It had taken all the courage I could muster to approach this man and in a moment he knocked my confidence so far back that it took me years before I would make myself vulnerable again. Instead of leaving that meeting with hope and determination, I left feeling condemned, confused, fearful and ashamed.

In my dream the people who came to see me after the attack sought to defend the lion. It is amazing how people will defend their own sin or the sin of others when it is confronted or challenged by the Holy Spirit.

How do you react when your areas of weakness are challenged? Personally, I hate people telling me I've been unjust or that I am wrong in my attitudes. My first reaction is nearly always to defend myself, even when I know I'm wrong. One night in a time of prayer, I asked God to show me the things that were holding me back from growing in my relationship with Him. God showed me my pride and judgmental attitude. I had lived with these attitudes for much of my life and not even seen them as wrong. I was shocked that God revealed these things to me. I thought he was going to show me some curse over my life or some demon that needed casting out. Instead he was saying, "Your wrong attitude means that the enemy can keep a hold on your life. Repent and he will lose his hold on you."

Suddenly, because I had asked God to work in me and show me the things that were offensive to him, He revealed to me what was really going on. I was stunned that I had been so wrong. "God forgive me" I prayed! Change me. I was so aware of how God hated the sin and yet loved me. And he did change me and I immediately became more gracious to others. These issues are often very subtle things, things that we may even consider just to be part of our character. Fortunately, Jesus is in the habit of changing our character. He loves us too much to leave us as we are.

Over the years I have realised that if I, in my position as a leader can't be honest about my struggles and hardships with the people I am leading then they feel inhibited to speak out about their own problems with me. Many times young men have come to talk to me about struggles in their lives and nearly every time they have said to me "Thank you for being honest, that's how I knew I could talk to you about this and that you wouldn't judge me." When I look back on my life, I wonder where

I would be if it wasn't for my Christian brothers who loved me and encouraged me in-spite of my honest confession of sin to them. God is awesome and faithful. He delights in us and longs for us to be honest with Him and with our Christian family about what is going on in our lives.

My hope in sharing this dream, is that we will pause and ask ourselves "what is holding my gaze? Is it Jesus or is it the lion that seeks to distract us from truly following Jesus?

Prayer
Here is a prayer that you can use as a guide to help you pray over the issues raised in this chapter.
Father, I thank you that you love me. That even in my sin you reached out to me. I want to be pleasing to you. Take my life and refine me. Show me the things that are offensive to you. Help me to acknowledge and change the things that keep me from your presence. I receive your forgiveness and I invite you to change my thinking and my behaviour. Refine me for your glory. Amen

Summary
The bible makes it clear that we have an enemy who seeks to lead us away from serving God. We need to be aware of his schemes and of the influence of sin in our lives. Jesus has defeated our enemy and has overcome the power of sin. We are able to live free from sin and it's influence on our lives.

We can overcome sin by:
Considering ourselves dead to sin - Saying no to sin - Allowing God to change our desires - Turning temptation to praise - Getting accountable to others - Breaking the strongholds - Redrawing the boundaries - Walking with the Holy Spirit.

When we choose to tackle sin and its influence in our lives we can enter into a time of spiritual battle, be encouraged, the opposition is a sign that we are provoking our enemy. As we continue to follow Christ our enemy will have to flee from us.

4. The Cemetery
God's Heart For The Prodigals

James 5:19-20
My brothers, if anyone among you wanders
from the truth and someone brings him back,
let him know that whoever brings back a sinner
from his wandering will save his soul from
death and will cover a multitude of sins.

When I was 17, I had the privilege of going to stay in the town of Chingola, in Zambia for several months. I was living with a missionary couple, Ben and Brenda Pitout, who were close friends of my parents. They had moved out to Zambia to establish a farm with the aim of training the local Zambian people in both farming and Christian ministry. I didn't know at the time that I would later take over this work. I had longed to visit Africa ever since receiving a call to missions at a young age and I was so excited to finally be on the mission field. I had come to Zambia to help Ben and Brenda in the early days of their ministry there. I spent most of my days on the farm, helping out in any way needed, in the evenings I had lots of time to read and pray. From time to time I would receive letters from family and friends back home.

One day I received a letter from my Mum back in England asking me to pray for two members of my family who were having a real tough time, neither of whom were walking with God at the time and they were both involved in drugs. It was the mid nineties and the rave scene was in full swing. My Mum's heart was broken for my family members and she longed to see a change to the destructive course they were on, one thing she knew for sure though was that God loved them and that he was the answer to reaching their hearts and minds. He was able to set them free and get them out of the danger they were in. "Please pray for them" she asked in her letter.

I sat down that night on my bed and as my mum had asked, I started to pray for my family members. I struggled to find the words to say but managed a simple prayer; "Lord Jesus, please help them, show them that what they are doing is the wrong thing." I felt like I was praying to just fulfil a religious duty. I had no desire in my heart to truly pray. Where was the passion? Why couldn't I get serious with God about this? It wasn't that I didn't care, just that I wasn't feeling a burden and I couldn't feel the heart of God for their lives. I knew I should want to pray but I just felt very apathetic. Feeling bad that I didn't care enough for my family, I changed my prayer and I simply asked God, "give me a burden for my family, show me how you see them." That at last was a sincere prayer from my heart. I realised that I needed God to change me so that I could pray in line with his heart. I soon went to bed. I had no idea that what would happen that night would totally change how I saw and felt for my loved ones.

———

That night, I dreamt I was walking down a street in my home town. I was following a beautiful woman ahead of me walking quickly down the street. I was intrigued by her and had a deep desire to know where she was going and why? The woman's eyes were glazed over and she didn't seem to be very aware of what was going on around her. It was like she was in a trance. She walked down the busy street ignoring all the people she was passing by almost as if she was unaware of their presence. The woman turned and walked through an open gate into a large cemetery. The cemetery was fenced off and the only access was through the gate she had entered. Intrigued, I followed about ten metres behind her. As I came into the grounds of the cemetery there was an uneasy feel in the air. It wasn't the clean well-kept cemetery I was used to but rather it was more like something out of a horror movie. It was oppressive with an evil feeling. I wondered what this beautiful woman was doing in such a horrible place. In the Cemetery the graves were open and corpses were laid on the ground inside the open graves. All the corpses were beginning to rot and the smell was almost unbearable. The sight made me want to run away and the smell was mak-

ing me nauseous. The woman however didn't seem fazed at all, in fact the environment seemed exciting to her. I watched as she walked up to a corpse; I was shocked to see her pick up the dead body and begin to caress it. "What are you doing" I asked, "Are you mad? That's a rotting body, you'll catch a disease." There was no response. I watched as the woman went to another dead body, picked it up and caressed it as if it were her lover. There was no response from the dead body and before long the woman moved on to another. Her clothes that had been pretty and fresh were now covered in rotten flesh and she stank of death and decay. The woman's face had been happy when she had entered the graveyard. As she had begun to play with the corpses, she had become almost ecstatic, as if she was getting real pleasure from her dead companions; but her eyes had been glazed over all along. She was in a dream world. She couldn't have been seeing the same thing as I was. I realised she was seeing an illusion. Now her face was changing, she was becoming frustrated and angry. The woman continued to play with the dead bodies even though she was not getting any pleasure from what she was doing. She was desperate to find something to satisfy her needs, but each new body just left her more and more distraught. I felt I was being torn apart inside, I had no power to intervene and the woman would not respond to me no matter how much I tried to reach her.

I was suddenly aware that I was no longer in the cemetery but rather I was standing in the middle of the road outside my parents' house, looking up at the house. A man was standing on the roof of the house with a gun in his hand. He too had the same glazed look on his face, that I had seen on the face of the young woman as she entered the cemetery. The man was firing the gun in the air, swinging his arm around, each time he did so the gun swung around by his head. One shot hit the road near me. Another just missed his head. I shouted to the man trying to calm him down but it had no effect and he went on as he was, unaware of the danger he was in and the danger he was placing others in around him.

————

About three in the morning, I woke up wet with perspiration, my heart pounding in my chest. Without even thinking I immediately fell to my knees beside my bed. My heart and thoughts for my family members were totally changed, I spent some time in real fervent prayer for them, weeping and crying out to God for their lives to be preserved and for their full salvation. God had answered my prayer and given me the burden I needed. There was another outcome of the dream though, not only was I now burdened to pray but I also had faith that God wanted to move in my family's lives. If this dream that God had given me in response to my prayer revealed how He saw them and how He felt for them, then surely if I and my family prayed in line with His desire, He would bring them back to himself. There are only a handful of times in my life that I have been so compelled to pray as I was that night. I was desperate. I realised the danger my loved ones were in; I understood the darkness that was gripping their lives and I knew that only God could make the difference needed to put them right.

It is easy to understand that the woman and man in my dream represented my family members. I didn't need much time to think to understand what the dream all meant. It was precise and to the point. Sometimes that's how God speaks to us, He makes things plain and simple so that we immediately know the answer to our request or question. At other times He gives us just part of the picture to draw us into searching out the meaning. I realised over time though that the man and woman didn't just represent those that I had a family bond with but the many that are wandering from God.

As I have thought about the dream over the years and have shared it with friends, God has shown me more and more truth hidden within the allegory of my dream.

Clothed In Fine Garments
I realised that both the people in my dream had been clothed in good clothes, they were not naked

or dressed in rags. This meant that they were loved by someone that had provided for them by giving them good clothes. I felt God was showing me that this meant they didn't represent the lost so much as they did those that had walked away from the family of God's people. I began to understand that they had been children within God's household. In the bible, garments are used as a picture of blessing, belonging, anointing and salvation. The priests that served in the tabernacle and later in the temple, were clothed with "holy garments". Joseph was beloved by his father more than his brothers and so his father had a coat of many colours made for him. When the prodigal son returned, his father told the servants to bring out the best robe and put it on him. *Isaiah (61:10)* says:

> *"I will greatly rejoice in the Lord;*
> *my soul shall exult in my God, for he has*
> *clothed me with the garments of salvation,*
> *he has covered me with the robe of righteousness,"*

In this passage, Isaiah is giving us a prophetic picture of what Jesus would do many years later. It tells us that we, as God's redeemed children, are clothed in salvation and righteousness. The image used here is of a dress or robe placed on us. In *Zachariah (3:3-5)* we read the account of Joshua, who at the time was high priest to the Israelites, we are told that his old filthy garments were taken off and he was clothed in new garments:

"Now Joshua was standing before the angel, clothed with filthy garments. And the angel said to those who were standing before him, "Remove the filthy garments from him."
And to him he said, "Behold, I have taken your iniquity away from you, and I will clothe you with pure vestments." And I said, "Let them put a clean turban on his head." So they put a clean turban on his head and clothed him with garments. And the angel of the Lord was standing by."

This picture given to Zachariah was specifically for Joshua the high priest, but it is also a picture to us of how the Holy Spirit finds us in our filthy rags and calls us to become priests to our God. He gives us garments fit for the task we are called to. He anoints us and equips us for service.

The man and woman in my dream were likewise clothed in fine clothes. They were children of a fine home, they were not orphaned or neglected. This revealed to me that they represented prodigals. They had been brought up in truth and provision but had run from their Father's house, leaving the care and provision that had been made available to them. They had traded the security and blessing of the family of God to pursue the fleeting pleasures of this world. They were dressed in fine clothes but were gradually turning their garments of righteousness into filthy rags.

In Revelation we find the message for the church in Sardis given to John. The beginning of the message is a strong rebuke to the church but the passage ends with a message of hope. Twice in the passage garments are mentioned. In *Revelation (3:4-5)* we read:

"Yet you have still a few names in Sardis,
people who have not soiled their garments, and
they will walk with me in white, for they are worthy.
The one who conquers will be clothed thus in white
garments, and I will never blot his name out
of the book of life. I will confess his name
before my Father and before his angels."

The image given us in this passage of soiling garments is quite blunt. Jesus' message to the church in Sardis was that some of them had not polluted their garments, meaning that many others had polluted their garments. Christ has clothed us in righteousness and we are to honour what He has given to us. Unfortunately far too often, rather than honouring that righteousness we return to the sin that we have been saved from. Returning to or continuing in sin causes God's gift of righteousness to us to be defiled. Righteousness is the garment placed on members of the church in Sardis, but their behaviour had stained the righteousness as muck would stain a pure white garment. When God's children continue in sin, they defile the splendid robes that He has given them.

This picture is a real challenge to us. We have been given something that we could never afford to buy, something that no amount of service could ever earn. Righteousness is the most precious thing we will ever receive and it cost Christ Jesus His life for us to receive it. How do we treat the garment of righteousness that He has given us? *Philippians (3:9)* tells us clearly that we have a righteousness given as a gift from God that comes through faith in Jesus Christ. When we sin we don't just draw away from God, we soil the garment of righteousness that He has given us.
Romans (3:22-24) puts it this way:

*"the righteousness of God through faith in
Jesus Christ for all who believe. For there is no
distinction: for all have sinned and fall short of the
glory of God, and are justified by his grace as a gift,
through the redemption that is in Christ Jesus,"*

As we saw from *Revelation 3* we are called to keep our righteous garments clean and not defile them.

Those represented in my dream, weren't just churched with religious ideas but had had a true knowledge of God in their lives. They had been clothed in God's love and righteousness. They knew he was real. They weren't orphans but children of God. Something though had gone wrong, they had been enticed away from their spiritual home, they had left the home of their loving Father and maybe just like the prodigal son believed the lie that he wouldn't want them back. It must grieve the heart of God to see His children walking away, becoming blinded by the things of this world. They leave the safety of the house of God, lured away by the attractions of the world, maybe they feel church is dull and out of touch with their lives. Maybe they have been hurt and rejected by their Christian family. Maybe rebellion has taken hold of their heart and they have decided to go their own way. There can be many reasons for people to walk away from the church family and from their Father God. To be honest I don't know what the reason was in my family members' case. I'm not sure even they did, but somehow they had gone from the place of his protection and love to a place of chasing fulfilment in things that would never truly satisfy them. They were dulling their senses and soiling their garments more and more.

It is so hard for families and churches to see their loved ones wander from their faith. I'm sure it is very hard for any parent to see their children on a destructive path. They can be good parents and bring up their children to walk with God. It is important to say that as parents we must guard against guilt that would try to overcome us if our children choose to walk away from following Christ. Each of us must bear the responsibility for our choices. We can't blame others for the choices that we make but that however doesn't mean that the circumstances around us don't play a powerful role in the choices we make.

When Jesus told the story of the prodigal son, He gave no reason for the son choosing to ask for his father's inheritance or for subsequently leaving the father's house. The prodigal was raised by a loving father but chose to go his own way leaving the security and provision of the family home to pursue his own way in life. Praise God that the father in the parable, just like our Father God, waited patiently with his arms wide open, to receive back his wayward son. There are though, some clear triggers for people walking away from faith and if we can understand some of these reasons then we can work to prevent them in our children, our family and in our churches. We can invite the Holy Spirit of God to change our hearts and to empower us to stand against anything that would seek to pull us or those around us away from Christ.

The prodigal
It can be hard to understand why people would walk away from their faith and relationship with Christ. Watching our loved ones walk away from faith in God is one of the hardest things that a de-

voted Christian can experience. For parents it can be very painful if their children choose that they no longer want to live as Christians and it may even cause them to fall out of good relationship with them. The example of the Father in the story of the prodigal son can be a great help to us in knowing how we relate to our loved ones in this circumstance. You can read the story in *Luke (15)*. It is worth noting that this is not a young child but a young man at a stage of life where he is able to make decisions for his own life and future. While we can pray and be an influence in our children's lives, we can only be responsible for them to the point that they are mature enough to make decisions for their own lives.

In the story, the younger son asked his father for his share in the father's inheritance. Some suggest that this would be the same as saying to his father, "I wish that you were dead so that I can enjoy what is yours now". Interestingly the father allowed the son to have the inheritance. He could have said 'no!' but he didn't. We can try and stand in the way of our children's freedom but that is not how the father in the story reacts and neither is it how our Heavenly Father acts. He allows us to make our own choices, He gives us freedom to abide with him or not. I am so grateful that my parents gave me a lot of freedom as a teenager and young adult. They put very little restraint on me and even allowed me to travel on mission trips in my teenage years. Seeking to control our children can breed contempt and alienate them. As our children grow it is important that we allow them to have more freedom and choice in life. I have seen many young people rebel against their parents because they felt their parents were too strict and controlling, we also see the opposite too where children are rude and rebellious because they lack boundaries. Finding a balance can feel like an impossible task. If you are a parent that struggles to know where the boundaries are, ask the Holy Spirit to give you grace and wisdom. He loves to empower us to be the best parents we can be.

The prodigal son leaves a few days later. The father does not insist that he remain at home. He allows his son to be free even though he knows that that freedom may lead him to ruin. The son soon gets himself into a real mess, he wastes all his money on foolish living and ends up caring for pigs. Pigs were an unclean animal to the Jews, the picture of a wealthy man's son now looking after unclean animals is a true fall from grace. Some would say he got what he deserved, he is suffering the consequences of his selfish actions. But the prodigal son's father doesn't say that! In *Luke (15:20)* we read about the father's heart toward his prodigal son;

> *"And he arose and came to his father.*
> *But while he was still a long way off,*

his father saw him and felt compassion,
and ran and embraced him and kissed him."

The father saw his son while he was still a long way off. It appears he was looking for his son's return. If we have prodigal sons and daughters, we must remember they are free to choose whose house they live in. We must look out for them though. I believe this looking out is a metaphor for us and represents standing in prayer. We are to look for our children's return to faith. Watching and praying for God to work in their hearts. Next the father runs to his son, kisses him and embraces him. He lavishes love on him. As parents there are three clear messages here for how we deal with our children.

1. Accept that they are free
Our children are not our possession. They have free will and must choose for themselves if they will follow Christ. We must do all that we can to lead our children into a choice to follow Jesus and I believe that parents that live lives of love for Jesus will see the fruit of that love in their children walking in right relationship with God.

2. Watch and Pray
Never give up on your children, fervently pray for their salvation. Keep watching. Let your love for them be united with God's heart for them and intercede for their lives. If you have young children

begin now to pray for them that they will love God and know His love in their lives. Pray that your children will have a deep and strong relationship with God and that they will never walk away from faith in God.

3. Welcome them home

One danger with prodigal children is that we become hard hearted or ashamed of them. The father in the story continued to love his son and as soon as he saw him returning, ran and did all he could to welcome him back home. That is exactly how God is to us. He did everything for us to come to him and when we did he lavished His love on us. God doesn't make us take the place of a servant in order to prove our worth to be accepted back. He embraces us and says, "you are my child and you have returned to your home, come enjoy the benefits of being my child." We need to receive our children in the same way.

What Creates A Prodigal?

In my dream I saw that the man and woman had been drawn away from the family. The woman in particular was searching for something that she felt was missing. It can help us to protect our children, both natural children and spiritual children, if we are aware of some of the things that may cause them to be led away from the spiritual home. Below are some areas that I have seen affect the spiritually young (young in the Christian faith) and the naturally young (young in years and maturity) and can lead them to walk away from relationship with God and His church.

Hypocrisy

It is heart breaking when I speak to young people that highlight hypocrisy for their reason to abandon their Christian Faith. While the truth may be that they are actually looking for an excuse, we mustn't underestimate the damage done by those that claim to be spiritual but live lives far from the reality of that spirituality. How sad that anyone in any church would feel this way. Hypocrisy kills trust. I have friends who were the children of parents in Christian ministry, that have struggled in their faith because they saw a different man or woman at home to whom they saw in the pulpit or on the stage on Sunday mornings. I have seen preachers that have laid themselves down for the church congregation but are angry and unloving toward their own children. As a father and a church minister my first and most important responsibility is to be authentic in my faith. I need to be godly not just in the eyes of my church but in my home where only my wife and children see me. I want my family to see me in church and say that the man they see preaching to the church is the same father and husband they see at home. As a minister of God's good news, I am called to display a standard not to just preach of one. Jesus hated hypocrisy and confronted the religious rulers of the day for their hypocrisy.

In *Luke (6:46)* Jesus says,

> *"Why do you call me, 'Lord, Lord,'*
> *and do not do what I say?"*

God is not just interested in our words and outward appearances. He is interested in the state of our hearts. He looks at the inner things, He wants us to form a genuine love for him and those around us, not an outer pretence of love. He desires lives that are obedient to what he says in public and in private.

I have had too many conversations with young Christians that are disillusioned with the church, their leaders and even their parents because what they see is not an authentic life lived for God. They long for godly men and women they can follow, that can lead and teach them by their lifestyle and not just their words but so often what they find at home or in private just doesn't match the image portrayed in public.

The point isn't that parents and leaders have to be perfect. That is just unrealistic. It is not perfection that God expects of us, rather it is honesty and humility. Hypocrisy isn't when we don't live up to the standard we aspire to. It is pretending to live up to that standard when we really don't. There is no room for hypocrisy in God's church. God knows we are not perfect, better than we know it ourselves, What's more our children know we are not perfect. God and our children are willing and able to forgive us our shortcomings and to be gracious toward us. However, if we present ourselves as better than we really are, then what will our children think of us? Worse still what will God think of us, presenting ourselves as something we are not? I for one, don't want my family to think I am perfect and I don't want my church to think I am perfect. On the contrary, I want them to know that I am a flawed individual who needs the grace of my Lord Jesus Christ day by day. I want them to know that I get it wrong, that I make mistakes, that I fail, but also that I rise up, shake off the dust and try again. I want them to know that their father, husband and minister gets it wrong just like they do and that he will understand when they make a mistake, that he will be gracious to them, just as they have been gracious to him. My wife and I agreed together when our children were very young that if we messed up with them that we would apologise to them and ask for their forgiveness. I have always tried to be honest with my children about my failings in life in order that they would be able to share with me their times of struggle and feelings.

Praise God we have a loving Father that will cleanse us and help us live differently. If you feel that others may have been negatively affected by seeing hypocrisy in your life, ask them for their forgiveness. Confess to them that you got it wrong. You may be amazed at the results.

Lack of love and Grace

When a Christian lacks love and grace we have to question if they have really understood the gospel. Over the years I have met with a number of Christians that were on the edge of walking away from their faith because they didn't see love and grace expressed among their Christian communities. Likewise, I have seen people won to faith in Christ because of Christians love and grace towards them. How wonderful when people are won to faith in Christ through the kindness of the people of God.

One day in conversation with one of my fellow pastors in our church. I mentioned to him a young man in the church that I hadn't seen for some months. "Has he gone to university" I asked. "No, didn't you hear! he has left the church and embraced a homosexual lifestyle" my friend replied. I was shocked. This had been a young man who had been very committed to the church and to following Christ. I found a contact number for the young man and asked if we could meet up. He was reluctant but willing to meet with me and we arranged to get together later that week for coffee and a chat. On meeting I could tell he was nervous to talk to me. We started with small talk for about twenty minutes and after he had relaxed and seemed less threatened, I asked him how he was doing and why I hadn't seen him at church for so long. He opened up and shared with me that for some years he had struggled with same sex attraction and that it had reached a point where he felt he couldn't continue as a Christian. I shared with him some of my own challenges that I had faced as a young man, hoping this would make him more comfortable to talk to me about his struggles. He told me that he hadn't felt able to share what he had been going through with anyone as all he heard from people in the church was negative and judgmental comments about homosexuality. I could feel his pain as I remembered how I had felt unable to share my own struggles as a youth, full of fear and shame at what others might think of me. Finally, he shared with me that the worst part for him was that he had heard his own family saying things like "homosexuals could not be Christians." He shared with me that he had struggled with his sexuality for a long time and had not overcome what he had seen as an inner battle, so now he had decided that the only choice he had was to embrace his sexuality, live as a gay man and believe that God didn't love or want him.

I couldn't believe that a young man in our church would come to this point, but I could relate to what he had gone through and felt a deep compassion for him. I had been in the same place years before but I thank God that I had found a different path and had known that God loved and wanted me. I had come to discover grace from

God, my family and my friends. I had been able to draw into God's loving arms rather than running away from Him. I tried to share God's love with this young man. I told Him that God loved him and that his struggle did not mean that he could not live a fulfilled life in relationship with God. I told him I would walk this path with him, but he was adamant he had made up his mind. As I walked back to my office that afternoon, I was so sad that this young man had walked away from pursuing God.

We must be careful not to lay the blame for people walking away from God on the church, we all make our own decisions in life, however, like this young man, it is often the perceived lack of love and grace from the church that contributes to some walking away.

God's love for us doesn't change even when we turn away from him, but our enemy looks for cracks in our relationship with God and our fellow believers to exploit and in this young man's case he had found an opportunity to force a wedge between him, his friends, his family, his church and his loving Heavenly Father. One of the tricks of the evil one is to make you feel isolated and to tell you that you are the only one going through trials and temptations. Sometimes it is convenient to blame others for our choices but it was true that people in the church had said things that had deeply hurt and rejected this young man. As James says in *James (3:6-10)*:

> "And the tongue is a fire, a world of unrighteousness. The tongue is set among our members, staining the whole body, setting on fire the entire course of life, and set on fire by hell. For every kind of beast and bird, of reptile and sea creature, can be tamed and has been tamed by mankind, but no human being can tame the tongue. It is a restless evil, full of deadly poison. With it we bless our Lord and Father, and with it we curse people who are made in the likeness of God. From the same mouth come blessing and cursing. My brothers, these things ought not to be so"

I wonder how much damage has been done due to careless words. As Christians we can't afford to be careless with our tongues as our words can push away those that need to be drawn near and embraced. We must always remember that it is the grace of God that brought us to himself, and we are to remain in that grace and likewise extend grace to those around us. In the story that I have shared about this young man it was harsh words and a judgmental attitude that caused offence and contributed to the justification he gave for walking away from Christ. The lack of grace that was shown was as much sin as the issue people were speaking against. It is crucial that we learn to be gracious in our speech and not cause unnecessary unwarranted offence.

Disillusionment

A third area that can draw people away from faith in Christ is disillusionment. This arises when we hear things promised that never come to pass. It is crucial that we don't just introduce young believers to a set of beliefs. While theology and teaching are of great value they are never meant to be received without the accompanying presence of the Spirit of God. My high school was a Christian school and one of the criteria for getting into the school was that you regularly attended church and were from a Christian family. So my whole school year had been brought up going to church or at least had attended for a few months in order to get a recommendation from the minister. However, in reality I would say less than a few dozen of them had any meaningful commitment to following Christ. Others may have believed in God but they were in no way disciples of Jesus. What went wrong? What was different for those that were seeking to live for Christ? I believe that for most of those in my school, church and Christianity was just a thing you did. No one had ever shown them what it meant to know Christ or to be led by the spirit. A powerless God that doesn't interact with them has no appeal whatsoever to most young people.

We can provide for our children, we can take them on camps, arrange fun activities and teach them well but none of this can compensate for a meaningful encounter with the living God. in *Proverbs (22:6)* we read that we should;

> *"train a child in the way he should go and when he is old he will not turn from it".*

The Hebrew word translated as "train up" is ḥânak̲. It's literal translation is 'to narrow' but we translate it as 'train up' or 'dedicate'. The literal translation though intrigues me! In English we sometimes talk about having a narrow focus meaning that we ignore other things and keep focused on the one crucial thing. So we can paraphrase this passage as 'Show your children how to focus, have their vision occupied by the way they should go and the way they should live (i.e. godly living and knowledge of what is true) and when they are old they will not get lost by wondering from the path.' The idea isn't just about teaching a child a set of truths but rather of discipling them by training them in what they need to do, like an apprentice learning from his mentor. We are not meant to bring up our children with just a knowledge about God. We are meant to train them by showing them the reality of God's character and authority. We need to train our children to know God not just know about Him but to experience

His presence and love for them. Concepts alone are not enough they need to see God demonstrated in the lives of their parents, teachers and church family.

So how do we train our children up in the way they should go?

1. By our example

In my twenties I worked as a youth leader in a number of different settings. On several occasions during this time, young people were sent to speak to me, because their parents felt they were rebellious and rude to their families. On a number of these occasions, I came to the conclusion that the children's bad behaviour was learned at home from the example their parents were setting. For example, one child's parent might say that their child was argumentative. When speaking to the child I heard from them that their parents often argued openly in front of their children. Our children learn behaviour from their parents. If the child has witnessed parents disrespecting one another or being unkind to other family members, then the child will feel within their rights to act in the same way. As parents we can't expect our children to behave in a way that we do not behave ourselves. 'Do as I say not as I do' is no way to train our children. Of course, children have their own character and will not always follow the example modelled to them by their family but parents need to take on board the responsibility of being the primary influence over their children's character and behaviour. Train them in the way they should go. In the same way if we want our children to be godly people then we need to set a godly model for them to follow.

There will be no greater joy for me in this life, than to see my children walking in close relationship with God. The only thing that could top that would be for them to say to me, "we learned this from you". Who I am and how I interact with my wife and children is one of the most important areas of my life. If I can live a Godly life in front of them then I can live it in front of anyone. What does your behaviour and your words teach your children? Do you display a life surrendered to the lordship of Christ? Or do your children see you as a different person in public to who they know you to be in private? Never underestimate the power of your example.

2. By introducing our children to the presence of God

Teaching our children to live moral lives helps to lay a great foundation for them to build their lives upon but a moral code and good conduct is no substitute for an encounter with God. We need to teach our children to encounter God. Our children need to know God's presence and power in their lives, not just stories of what he did a long time ago. This can sound like a big challenge to many of us. We may struggle to get into God's presence ourselves. How do we get our children there? The first step is to let your children see you entering in yourself. Talk to them about the wonderful things that have happened in your times with God. Tell them how He has changed you and the joy that you have received from him. Secondly ask God to help your children to experience Him. Thirdly put them in environments where the Holy Spirit is moving and where they can experience the presence of God and the miraculous for themselves. I remember one evening I was sitting in my office, playing my guitar and worshiping God. My son Zion who was 5 years old at the time, walked into the room. He had been put to bed already and so I was about to take him back to bed as it was well after his bedtime but I felt the Holy Spirit prompt me to invite him to join me. "Zion, you are meant to be in bed now, Daddy is spending some time with God, you can stay if you would like but it's not a play time, it's a worship time." He came in and sat on the floor. I continued to worship and was really aware of the sweet presence of God in the room. I was moved to tears as I sometimes am in times of intimate worship. After some time, I looked over at Zion, he was sitting quietly with his eyes closed. I could tell that God was moving in his heart. How wonderful that time was, just to know that through my devotional life my son got to experience God's presence. I remember when each of our children were little, I would hold them in my arms during the worship time at church. I would worship wholeheartedly and pray over them that they too would be worshipers. Are our homes places of spiritual warmth? Are they environments that invite the Holy Spirit's presence? If not, choose to make them so. Choose to seek God's presence in your home and where possible with your children.

A friend of mine once shared a story with me of a young girl she knew. This girl's mother was a really strong Christian and whenever the daughter faced problems she would go to her mother to pray for her. The mother would pray and the daughter's problems would be sorted out. Eventually the daughter went off to University. Within one year the daughter returned home pregnant and in a real mess spiritually. Her mother couldn't understand what had gone wrong. She felt that she had demonstrated a godly life to her daughter and now why was she in such a mess? The mother began to realise what the problem was, she had always done the praying that had lifted her daughter out of all her problems. The mother had never trained the daughter to pray for herself or shown her how to live in Christ herself. As long as the daughter had the mother with her, she was fine but when her prayer support and rock was removed the daughter had no knowledge how to go to God herself. The daughter didn't know how to overcome the pressures and temptations she faced. She didn't know how to bring those pressures and temptations to a loving God, mum had always done that for her.

Let's imagine that your child leaves home and lives in a home of their own. They will need to know how to practically care for the home, how to pay the bills, use the washing machine and how to keep the house clean. How do our children learn these things? They learn them through watching us and through doing these things with us. If your child's only experience of doing the laundry is to find clean clothes washed, ironed and folded at the end of the bed ready for them, then how are they to know what to do in their new home? They need to do it with us first so they can know how to do it alone. As in the natural so in the spiritual, we need to do it with them not just for them. This is how we equip them for life.

3. By protecting our children from controversy
It is surprising the things children hear and see, when no one notices they are there. We need to be careful to protect our children and young people from controversy and divisions in the family and in the church. Too often children and young people are victims of their parents' offences. When parents are offended and leave churches because of offence, or they were not willing to deal rightly with a conflict that had arisen the children are also stopped from going and being with their Christian friends. Where the parents may have the ability to keep their faith alive for a time on their own, often the children are not mature enough to do so. I believe if Christian parents

would consider their children more, then we would see far fewer youths walking away from the church. Out of my friends that I grew up with in church, most whose parents remained in the church through the years have grown up children that are now still walking with Christ. Of the families that left the church due to arguments and offence, most of their children are now not walking with Christ. Please don't misunderstand me. There are times when we have to walk away from a church due to unreconcilable issues or because the church leaders are not honouring God. This though should not be done lightly and if you believe it is necessary after seeking God and searching your own heart, then ensure that you get your children somewhere they will grow and be nurtured in their faith. I don't raise this point lightly, but it should be a wakeup call to parents. If you take your children away from a youth group of young people living for Christ and cause them to stop attending church, this could cause your children spiritual damage.

Please don't misunderstand me. I am not trying to lay guilt on anyone but rather to challenge us to be sure that we are not causing problems for our children because we are not willing to deal with our own pride and anger. If you are in a church environment that is controlling or there are unresolvable issues you don't need to stay and put up with it. No not at all. But don't walk away from a church family out of anger or rebellion. If you do have to walk away, do so prayerfully recognising that you need to put your children first as you decide what to do next. Seek God for his protection over your children. Get them into a good church as soon as possible and if possible be lovingly honest to them about the reasons. When choosing a new church think of their growth and development as important as your own.

4. Loving with the Fathers heart

The greatest lesson any leader or parent can learn is that our first responsibility is to demonstrate to those in our care who God is and what He is like. This principle applies to anyone in leadership too. We are to be imitators of God in our relationships with those in our care. By this I mean that we treat those we are caring for as God treats us. God is gracious and so we are to be gracious and teach others to be gracious too. God is a father that restores us when we have done wrong, so we should restore our children when they mess up and we should help our children to restore others. God is also a father that disciplines his children. Discipline doesn't mean beating people when they get it wrong but in love correcting them, not ignoring the small things but taking them aside and showing them the wrong, helping them to understand that they need to take responsibility for their words and conduct.

It may seem strange to you that I should even need to mention that we need to love. Surely that is the most obvious thing that any Christian in a position of care and leadership should do? Unfortunately, too often loving one another with the love of God is not an easy or instinctive thing to do. I have often heard from Christian leaders that they have so much grace for those that are not Christians but really struggle to have that same grace and compassion for members of their own church or ministry. Strangely this can also be the case in some families. As a child, I was once at a friend's house for tea. While the father was in the kitchen getting a dish for the table, I accidentally knocked over the jug of water on the table. The jug was full and the water went everywhere. As the father returned into the room and saw the mess, he flew into a rage at his children, demanding to know who had done this. Fearfully I told the father that I was the one that had knocked over the jug. In a moment his demeanour totally changed and he began to tell me that it was no problem and that accidents happen. I have seen this same attitude in ministry, where the ministry leader will do anything for those they are caring for or seeking to reach with the gospel but will treat their team with very little grace and patience.

I am aware as I am writing this that it may sound like I think that I have got it all together and that my children are perfect model children that love Jesus and their family unconditionally. Don't be fooled! As a family we are a long way from getting all this right. I am not a perfect father but praise

God, I have the spirit of God and He is training me as I seek to be the image of Christ to my family.

What do those around us, see in us? Are we what we want them to be or are we hoping they won't turn out like us. I worked with young people for some years, and in that time I often saw that if parents were insecure, fearful or aggressive these traits would surface in their children. Likewise, where parents were generous and peaceful their children often reflected these characteristics too. As a parent, I now see in myself many behaviour patterns I observed in my own parents. Most I thank God for, a few I pray He will change in me. It is no good for me to say "I don't want my kids to turn out like me!" I need to say "I will change and keep changing till I want my children to be what they see in me." Paul writing to the Corinthians in 1 Corinthians (11:1) says

"Be imitators of me, as I am of Christ."

What a bold statement. It sounds almost arrogant but that is the commitment Paul had to the church. He wasn't just a follower of Christ for his own good but also to show the church how to live. We are to live lives of service and love in the sight of others in such a way so as to show how they themselves ought to live for Christ.

I believe it is parents' responsibility to lead their children into a commitment to follow and serve Christ. We are not to leave this most beautiful gift to others or expect it to be the responsibility of the church's youth or children's workers. I am so grateful that years ago when I came home from a midweek children's meeting, where the gospel message was shared. I brought back the questions I had about salvation to my mum and dad. My parents sat down with me and explained things to me and led me through to a full understanding of salvation. As I write this I am full of joy as I remember that night. I am so thankful to God for my parents, they have been to me a model of godliness to follow, they trained me in the way I should go and I am not going to depart from it. I'm not saying they were perfect parents, who is? But they did not leave me just to find my own way, they showed me the way in which I should walk. Thank you Mum and Dad, thank you God for this blessing.

Some Christian parents response to their children walking away from God is to be apathetic, they may think it's just a phase their children are going through. I remember when I was at Bible school someone posed the question "why do so many young people leave the church?", a classmate responded "Its natural for kids to rebel." I was so angry, not with my classmate but with the attitude he was expressing. If we expect our kids to struggle in their faith and rebel, then it is very likely they will. To me, this is such a wrong way to think and in fact it is contrary to the promise we read earlier, that if we train our children in the way they should go they will not depart from it. Our expectation should be that our children will continue in faith all their days. We should believe for it, we should pray for it and we should do all that we can to see if happen. We should teach our children the stories of David who in his youth spent his time in the presence of God. Daniel, who, though he was taken away from his land, his family and his temple and although he could live on the choicest of foods and fine wines, held to what he knew was true, making a vow before God not to defile himself. While it is true that some young people do walk away from God because they are rebelling, I am convinced that for the vast majority, they do so because they don't see in reality what they read about in the bible and because they don't see lives living out what they have been taught. Young people are hungry for reality and freedom but often what they are offered in their local church is dead tradition, rules, control and hypocrisy. What they need to see is a family that loves them and rejoices over them, supporting them in their tough times and celebrating them in their triumphs.

In our church when I was a child, the things of God, spiritual gifts, prophecy, signs, wonders and miracles were not just for the adults. We were encouraged to pursue these things and as I saw them

I was more and more convinced of my God, His goodness and of my desire to live a life committed to Him.

Blinded

The eyes of the woman in my dream had made her look like she was in a trance, this showed me that she was not really seeing the reality of what was going on around her. She was blinded to the sin and danger she was in. She was seeing things that weren't there, not seeing the things that were real, she was perceiving things to be different than they really were. The corpses were so attractive to the woman that she flung herself at them yet in reality they were decaying bodies. God was showing me not only the state of my loved ones, but He wanted to show me how important it is to see sin as He sees it. If we could see sin with God's eyes, as it really is, not as the world portrays it, then how different our attitude would be toward it. If we truly understood the filth and power of sin then we may think twice about entering into it.

When I was 21 I spent some time in India, with two of my closest friends. We were on a world tour and each of us had chosen countries we wanted to visit. India had been one of my choices as I had never been there but I had always wanted to visit. One night as we walked along a street in the heart of Mumbai I saw a woman begging. She looked very young, I thought between 15 and 17 years old. She was very pretty but had a worn face.

She carried a baby in her arms and I assume it was her own child; she seemed to be homeless, living on the streets like many people in Mumbai. As I walked past I saw the woman's eyes, they had the same look as the women's in my dream, they were glazed over, there was a weird smile on her face, the baby seemed to have glazed eyes too. It is the look you might get from being high on drugs and only partly aware of what is happening around you. The woman's behaviour too confirmed to me that she was high. I was so saddened by what I saw, the baby couldn't have been more than a year old, and it seemed to me was already affected by its mother's addiction to drugs. Unfortunately, there are many young women like this. Not just in Mumbai but all over the world, exploited and controlled by addiction and far too often by those that wickedly lead them into addiction. In a sense everyone without Christ is like this woman. Looking for joy in the next thing to come along, only to find themselves further and further from true joy that is only found in the freedom that Christ brings.

God doesn't want us to be ignorant of our enemy's schemes. The enemy seeks to get a hold on our young people by putting something in front of them to entice them into sin, even though they have been told it is wrong, they enjoy this new thing and before long they're hooked, simple but effective. The enemy's schemes haven't changed in thousands of years, they were the same in the time of Samson as they are today as illustrated by Samson's story in *Judges (13-16)*.

Samson was chosen by God to save his people from the Philistines. Let's look at what the angel told his mother in *Judges (13:2-6)*.

"There was a certain man of Zorah, of the
tribe of the Danites, whose name was Manoah.
And his wife was barren and had no children.
And the angel of the Lord appeared to the woman
and said to her, "Behold, you are barren and have
not borne children, but you shall conceive and bear
a son. Therefore be careful and drink no wine or
strong drink, and eat nothing unclean, for behold,
you shall conceive and bear a son.
No razor shall come upon his head, for the
child shall be a Nazirite to God from the womb,
and he shall begin to save Israel from
the hand of the Philistines."

Samson's mother had been unable to have children and now the angel had told her not only that she would have a child but that this child would be an instrument of God to save his people. How much joy this must have brought to Samson's parents. There were however requirements of them. They were to bring Samson up as a Nazarite. When Samson's mother told her husband about this visitation he sought God to allow the angel to come again so they would know how they should bring up their child.

"Then Manoah prayed to the Lord and said,
"O Lord, please let the man of God whom you
sent come again to us and teach us what we
are to do with the child who will be born."

Judges 13:8-9a

What wisdom. To ask God to show them the way to parent their child, we could learn so much from their example. And so Samson's parents taught him the rules, how he should live as a Nazarite one of which was that, he was not to cut his hair. Something went wrong for Samson though. As a young man he ceased to follow the instructions that were given to him. We can't lay the responsibility for this at the feet of his parents as it seems from the story that they did all that was asked of them, but something wasn't right with Samson. He had an unhealthy appetite for the Philistine women and before long he was in the arms of Delilah, the woman that would lead to his downfall. So what went wrong for Samson? It seems his enemy found his weakness and used it against him to cause him to compromise and that is exactly what the enemy of our soul seeks to do in our lives. He looks for weakness, things he can exploit to separate us from our family, to isolate us and finally to cause us to pursue things that lead us away from serving God. When we look at Samson we see that he was not among his family but was spending more and more time with a Philistine woman, a woman who didn't serve his God and didn't have his interest at heart. He was separated, isolate, enticed, weakened and all this led to his captivity.

We can see the enemy's strategy again and again in the lives of believers being pulled away from God's family and from relationship with Jesus. Let's look at these three steps and see how we can overcome them.

1. Separated

First our enemy seeks to separate us from God's people. Maybe you have heard the voice that tells you, "you don't fit in here", "no one understands you", "you're not like them". It is the voice of the evil one that wants God's people to divide, to push us away from fellowship. He may tell us that we don't fit in at church, everyone here is so holy and you're still a sinner. I have served in churches with some of the most caring people I have met anywhere and yet met with people in those churches that will tell me "this church is so unloving", "nobody cares for me here". Now I know that sometimes people can be unloving but most times when I hear these kind of statements, I recognise that I am hearing the voice of the enemy that has been lying to my brother or sister in order to separate them from the family of Christ. I too have been influenced by these same lies in the past, I've heard the voice that told me, "you're different from them, no one here would understand what you're going through" and to my sorrow I believed the voice rather than believing my Heavenly Father who says I am part of his body, part of his family, even in my failings. In Christ we are members of one another, we need his family around us to truly live the life God has called us to.

2. Isolated

When we begin to listen to that voice we separate ourselves off from our Christian family. We don't go to church, we don't meet with Christian friends and we even begin to stop our godly habits. Prayer is not a pleasure anymore but rather a burden. The bible is uninteresting and disconnected. And the sweet presence of Christ is a distant memory. Before long we have no one to turn to, no one to confide in and we are isolated.

3. Enticed

In this place of isolation, we begin to long for what we have lost. We want a family around us; companions and a sense of belonging. This is where the enemy will step in again and try to lead us into unhealthy relationships. Suddenly the idea of what would have once been abhorrent to us becomes attractive and we are enticed away from devotion to Christ, seeking to meet our need to belong wherever we can.

If we can understand this strategy of our enemy then we can prevent ourselves and our loved ones from being drawn away from God and his people.

To illustrate this patten I want to tell you a story of a friend of mine. For the sake of this book some of the details have been changed to protect their identity and respect their privacy.

My friend was brought up in a Christian home. Everyone thought her parents were wonderful Christians but those of us who know her well knew that the parents were not as loving as they appeared. My friend grew as a follower of Jesus and had great encounters with the love of God. She loved her bible and she loved Jesus. She had many friends at church and enjoyed being an active part of the youth group. In her later teenage years my friend began to see a non-Christian boy. She confided in one of her girlfriends from church and her friend told her not to pursue the relationship because she felt the boy had bad intentions and that it would be a mistake and that she could see that her desire for this young man was already affecting her relationship with God. Over the next few months we noticed that our friend was at church less and less. She had begun to separate herself from her Christian friends. She wasn't happy with them because they didn't support her choice to go out with this boy. She was now separated. Before long, her new boyfriend began to push her to have sex with him. I remember many times my friend had told me she was saving herself for marriage and how she didn't feel she would be able to marry a man that had not done the same. Normally at this point my friend would call her Christian friends for help and prayer but she had separated herself from her friends. She began to feel alone. She missed being part of a fun and exciting church family. She was now isolated and in a perfect spot for the hunter (the devil) to pick her off. Feeling lonely and isolated pushed her to agree to sleep with her boyfriend. She was enticed by the idea of being close to someone, being loved and wanted by someone. And so she did, she gave this boy her most prized possession, she gave him her virginity. She told me later that that night she had felt such shame. Not many weeks later the boyfriend left her, and she was spiritually and emotionally shattered. When I met with her sometime later she told me that from that time she had begun to believe that God would not want her back and that her friends would despise her for what she had done. Neither were true but these lies caused her to withdraw even more.

This is an example that includes losing sexual purity, but the same story is repeated in many ways. If our enemy can separate us then he is half way to his ambition of causing us to be broken and ashamed. This is what he seeks to do in our lives, he seeks to separate us, isolate us, entice us and his desire is to destroy us. It is also what he did in

Samson's life. But, praise God, that is not the end of the story.

It wasn't until Samson had had his eyes gouged out and he was living as a slave of the Philistines, that he was restored. We read what happened in *Judges (16:28-30)*.

"Then Samson called to the LORD and said,
"O Lord GOD, please remember me and
please strengthen me only this once,
O God, that I may be avenged on the Philistines
for my two eyes." And Samson grasped the two
middle pillars on which the house rested,
and he leaned his weight against them,
his right hand on the one and his left hand on
the other. And Samson said, "Let me die with the
Philistines." Then he bowed with all his strength,
and the house fell upon the lords and upon all the
people who were in it. So the dead whom he
killed at his death were more than those
whom he had killed during his life."

This restoration led to his greatest victory over his enemies. Praise God that wherever our children may be at right now they too have an ending to their story and like Samson it can be one of victory over their enemy.

Now that we have seen these stages of attack from the enemy, let's consider how we can help someone in the midst of those stages.

Combating separation, isolation and enticement

Firstly it is crucial that we recognise our role as leaders or parents is not just to try and persuade those we care for to think and behave differently, we want to birth in them a realisation of who God is and who they are in him. We recognise though that we are in a spiritual battle for their heart and mind. Prayer is always our first priority when we see a brother or sister withdrawing from relationship with God and his people. Pray for their eyes to be opened. Pray for yourself to have wisdom, love and courage. Pray for the Holy Spirit and God's angels to protect and to reveal truth to the loved one. Next pursue them. Consider it your honour to win them back to God. In *James (5:19-20)* we read;

> *"My brothers, if anyone among you wanders*
> *from the truth and someone brings him back,*
> *let him know that whoever brings back a sinner*
> *from his wandering will save his soul from*
> *death and will cover a multitude of sins".*

It is no small thing to bring back a wanderer from God's family. Let the loved one speak. We need to give them opportunity to express themselves and we need to be caring and patient with them. Be firm though and challenge where you can see they have believed a lie from the evil one. Encourage them no matter how far they may have wandered, that God's arms are still open to them and so are the arms of his people. Being vulnerable, sharing our weaknesses and failings can be a great encouragement to others, as they realise that they are not the only ones to struggle and make mistakes.

Don't give up, often we reach out to loved ones a few times and when they don't respond we stop trying. We need to be like Christ in this matter. Jesus doesn't stop chasing after us when we wonder off and He doesn't take NO for an answer. We can walk away and close ourselves off to Him again and again, but He still comes after us. Keep the door open, keep inviting people, keep praying.

We also need to demonstrate grace and mercy when we see others caught in sin. This doesn't mean that we ignore the sin but we still love the person and we help them to know that they are always welcome back.

Our aim is not to judge but to lovingly and graciously lead people to seek forgiveness and restoration.

Love is the motivation

As Christian parents, leaders or church family we need to introduce our children, both young people and those young in their faith, to the reality of who God is, His love, His presence and His power. We are not to just tell our children the stories about him. Our children need to know Jesus, to understand that he loves them and that following Him is not just keeping rules. If we bring up our children to serve God out of fear alone then we have missed the point of the gospel. We want our children to serve and honour God out of a heart of love for what he has done for and in them.

I am convinced that a life motivated and empowered by love will live for God and overcome all opposition while a heart motivated by fear and laws will fail to sustain a right relationship with God.

I believe that if children respect their parents then they will obey them. The same goes for their relationship with God. If we have a revelation of God's love for us then we can in turn love God, that love for him causes us to want to respect and obey him. Learning rules alone can never achieve this. We must set the example; we cannot expect others to respect God if we don't do so ourselves. "Blazing fires spread, embers die out". I have seen some young people head away from the Lord and their parents say nothing, they are worried about putting pressure on their kids, but I say by not challenging our children we are often encouraging them in their rebellion against God. So what am I saying? That if your children aren't following God that it is your fault? No, this is not true, every child makes their own choices and as parents we cannot take sole responsibility for our children's actions, but often we take no responsibility at all. We don't take our role seriously. Too many parents don't even have meaningful conversations with their children. If only Fathers could learn to share their struggles and weaknesses with their sons they would be amazed how their sons would open up to them and how much deeper their relationship would be. Being a Christian parent is not only about the ability to father or mother our children it's also about disciplining yourself and poring yourself out so that your children may learn from you and be all that God calls them to be. I once heard a preacher say that "in the West, Christians are more worried about their children being happy than about them being righteous." We need to be serious with God about our family members that are not serving him. Ask God to give you an understanding of how He sees them. Ask Him to give you a burden for their salvation.

If you feel that your actions may have contributed to a loved one walking away from following Jesus, confess it to God and ask his forgiveness. He is faithful to forgive us and will not hold your mistakes against you. Guilt is not from God and brings nothing but pain. You can also ask the forgiveness of the child or friend you are thinking of. Pray for them and ask God to restore them.

Prayer

Here is a prayer that you can use to help you pray for your loved ones; Lord, open our eyes, don't let us be blind to sin and it's power against us, but let us see with your vision and understand with your heart. Let the powers of the enemy be disgraced and fall back from your children, give us the grace and wisdom to lead those in our care in the paths of righteousness and help us show Christ to them. Let the prodigals return to your home. Let us be a church that loves them. For the glory of Your wonderful name. Amen.

Summary

Jesus made it clear that there is grace for the prodigal. He desires all to come to a knowledge of his love for them, to abide in his house. As leaders, parents and Christian brothers and sisters, we should see the responsibility of bringing home the prodigals as our own. We can also work to help prevent prodigals ever leaving by creating an authentic loving culture and dealing with hypocrisy in our churches   and families. Recognise the enemy's plan to 'Separate', 'Isolate' and 'Entice' our family members. Ask God to give you a heart for broken Christians as much as a heart for the broken world. We can work to be an example to

those we care for, introducing them to the presence and love of God.

5. Into The Fire
A call to evangelism

Matthew 16:15
"And he said to them, "Go into all the world and proclaim the gospel to the whole creation".

Through the 1990s our church in Croydon ran a series of mission trips to Eastern Europe. We would join with long term mission partners in proclaiming the gospel through street outreach and tent meetings. Alongside these we would get involved in serving the community through social action projects. We would travel by bus from London all the way through France and Germany and end up somewhere in the Czech or Slovak republics. As young people these trips were great fun. I had little real understanding at the time of just how significant the changes that had been taking place in this part of the word had been for the former communist countries. At the time there was a great response from Eastern Europeans to these crazy western Europeans dancing, singing and acting in their town squares and outside their public buildings. We definitely had the novelty factor. I was involved in the worship and drama teams and on rare occasions even joined the dance group. I am not sure why they allowed me to dance as I could never get the steps right, my friend would often have to call out the next steps to me as we went through the dance routine. Over the years these trips had a great effect on myself and on many of my friends, shaping our character while also causing us to be grateful to God for the freedom to worship that we had experienced growing up in Britain. It was great, in some small measure, to be helping the churches we were working with to engage their community with the gospel message. It was a privilege to serve on these trips and it helped to unite us and build our faith to see people coming to Christ as we gave ourselves to serve the churches in Eastern Europe. On one of the last trips we did to the Czech Republic though, it felt that our team was having a lot of trouble. Some of the young people on the trip were constantly bickering and it felt that some of the team saw this more as a summer holiday than a mission trip.

Unlike previous trips the crowds didn't gather to watch and listen to us and we were having long days in the sun with very little result. When we were not doing street evangelism, most of our time and energy seemed to be taken up with listening to people's gripes and petty squabbles. It felt more like a high school exchange trip than a mission trip. Every day someone else was falling out with one of their friends. The devil was having a field day with us and we were totally ineffective. There seemed to be very little grace among our team. Rather than the love of God shining through our lives and winning people to Christ, we were under a shadow of darkness that was affecting our attitudes and causing us to be anything but a godly witness. I felt our bad character and lack of love was more likely to repel people from the gospel than to attract them to receive Christ. What kind of witness are we being? I asked myself. One night as I was praying, I asked God "What are we doing here? What is the point of all the work we have put into this trip if all the team is going to do is fall out and bicker? God we are totally ineffective here, what is going on?". Looking back now I can see that many of our team were immature in their faith and some were not living lives surrendered to Christ. That same night I had a dream.

— — —

I was myself standing in the attic of my parent's house in the south of France; 'Pleasant Places', the house's name, had served as a base from which my parents could visit and minister to churches in the southwest of France as well as being our family holiday retreat, since I was 11 years old. We would spend our summer and easter holidays there.

For me, this old house in the mountains, was my

real home. I felt more of a connection to it than I did to our house in Croydon. When traveling the world in my late teens and early twenties, I would speak to my parents and not really miss home too much but when I knew that my family were at our house in France I would become homesick and feel the distance strongly. That house was my true home and it held fond memories for me of great times I had spent there with family and friends. Things just didn't feel right if I was unable to visit Pleasant Places for a long time. Even today, the thought of our family home stirs strong emotions for me.

The house, a stone building, is set in the beautiful mountain countryside of the Northern Ardeche surrounded by hills covered in pine forests. The house is built on a hillside, so that the attic opens up onto flat ground at the back of the house, the first floor opens on flat ground to the side of the house and the living room on the ground floor opens up on to flat ground at the front of the house. Behind the house is a forest of pine trees, where, as a teenager I would build tree houses with my brothers and our friends and where we would spend many hours climbing trees and playing hide and seek.

In my dream I was standing in the attic of the house, the attic was filled with people from my church and many of my friends who were with me on our mission trip were also present. The house felt safe and warm and was filled with a feeling of peace and calm. There was a tangible sense of God's presence around us. I was aware of a wonderful feeling of being with family and knew that I was loved and cared for by the people in the house. The whole atmosphere was like you would expect among a group of people that truly care for one another and enjoyed each other's company. Suddenly the peace of the house was disturbed by cries for help coming from behind the house. Some people didn't seem to notice the sound at first but I could hear it clearly and was unsettled at what I heard. A group of us ran over to the door of the attic that opened at the back of the house. Opening the door we looked outside to see what was wrong. From the safety of the house, we could see the forest behind had caught fire, we could make out the figures of people trapped within the flames. It was these people trapped in the fire that we could hear, they were crying for help.

We turned to the others in the house and called out, "There is a fire in the forest and there are people trapped among the trees". "We must do something to help them", someone called to the church in the attic. The group of us at the door quickly decided to go into the fire and try to rescue those in trouble. As we prepared to go out of the door, some of the people in the house started to get concerned. "Wait a minute" one said, "there isn't enough room to bring in lots more people in here", "their wounds will cause disease to come into our home" said another, others joined in, "you'll get hurt if you go out there", "we don't know those people and we don't know their intentions". I couldn't believe my ears. Did they really expect us to leave people to die in the fire without trying to help them? Some of the group that were going to go out began to get discouraged and said "maybe we shouldn't go if isn't safe," "we don't want to get burned as well".

Suddenly I felt an anger building up inside me. Were we really debating whether or not we should help those in need? Behind us, outside the house, the shouts for help were becoming more desperate and I couldn't bear it any longer. "Doesn't the Bible teach us that we will walk through fire and not be burned, through water and not drown, we must go!" I said. "How can we not care for those in need". Encouraged by God's promise from His word a group of us left the house and headed into the forest. The forest was now completely engulfed in flames, and it was not easy to see where we were going through the smoke and distortion of the flames. We followed the cries of those trapped in the fire. As we found them we were able to embrace them and lead them quickly out of the burning forest and into the attic of the house. Although the smoke from the fire made it hard to see and the flames were hot, neither the flames nor the smoke caused our group of rescuers any harm, it was as if our bodies became fireproof and our lungs unaffected by the smoke.

As time went on we were able to save many people from the fire, bringing them one by one into the house. The wounds on some of the people we had rescued were horrendous, we prayed for them and dressed their wounds as best we could. After some time in the house their wounds began to heal. We were shocked at how fast this had taken place, especially as some of the people who had been in the house many years had wounds that had never really healed. Why were these newcomers receiving healing from being in the house while others after many years in the house had not improved at all? Some of those that had tried to stop us going out into the fire were not happy with the new arrivals. It cost us much time, energy, space and wealth to rescue and care for them. We continued to bring in the wounded, in spite of the discouragements we faced from our church family and eventually we had brought everyone we could find out of the fire and into safety. That was when I woke up.

— — —

I woke up around 4am aware that God had responded to my question, He had shown me what we were doing in eastern Europe and how important the work we were doing really was. In the morning, I felt that my focus and passion for the trip had been restored. We were here to save the lost, from the fire of sin that seeks to take their lives, and bring them safe into the house of God, into His family. We had all that was needed to rescue, heal and provide for these people, God had allowed us to hear their call for help and He had sent us out to bring in His lost children. The dream challenged me to get my focus back on our true mission and gave me a real desire to pray for the unity of our team. I felt I had new insight into how God saw the lost and how the church could grieve His heart when it didn't walk out the call He had given it. I saw that the very people called to make Christ known could be hostile to the idea of opening the church doors to the lost.

I shared my dream with some of the team and we began to pray for God to help us refocus on his mission. We also prayed against the lies and entanglements of the enemy that had been distracting some of our team from what we were here to do. From that day things began to change. The team began to deal with the petty issues that had been dividing us and relationships were restored. The dream also gave me resolve not to get caught up in silly arguments and distractions. There will always be those that seek to distract and prevent us from walking out what God has called us to do. Our job is to choose not to allow ourselves to be distracted but to get on with the task set before us.

Before we look at why and how the church needs to return to its call to reach the lost let me say honestly that evangelism has always been an area that I have found very difficult. I am a long way from being an effective evangelist, so this dream is the one that is the greatest challenge to me at this time in my life and the principles here are ones I need to embrace as much as anyone else. It is peculiar that I have very little problem preaching and sharing my heart with large crowds of people but in conversation with just one non believer I find it so hard to share my faith openly. Over the years I have been tempted to excuse this by saying this is because "I am a bible teacher not an evangelist" or "I'm called to the church not the lost". But when I search my heart honestly and openly, these arguments are an excuse for not walking in obedience to Christ. We are not all evangelists but we are all called to be witnesses. In *1 Peter (3:15)* the bible tells us;

> *"but in your hearts honour Christ the Lord*
> *as holy, always being prepared to make a*
> *defence to anyone who asks you for a reason*
> *for the hope that is in you; yet do it with*
> *gentleness and respect,"*

Being ready to share our faith is crucial if we are to be the people God has called us to be, achieving the commission He has called us to achieve.

Through my dream God helped me see that we had forgotten our reason for being in Eastern Europe, I believe that one of the greatest challenges facing churches today is that in all their good works they forget the reason that God sent us into the world. The ministry of reaching the lost is both the greatest challenge and blessing given to the church. In this chapter we will see how all of God's people, not just those with a specific call to be evangelists are called to reach the world with God's gospel of salvation.

Returning to the commission

Let's begin by dispelling the notion that we can choose whether we should engage with evangelism or not. It seems to me that western Christians in particular are guilty of engaging with the aspects of God's church that we enjoy and neglecting the parts we don't. Evangelism is one of those areas that many of us never consider engaging in. We choose to leave it to the professionals or the nut jobs on the high street corner. Many of us have never look for or prayed for an opportunity to share our faith with our neighbours or loved ones and we will find all sorts of reasons not to see evangelism as something we should do. Maybe you have never been told it is your responsibility; this is quite possible because it is not just individuals but also whole churches that ignore the call to make Christ known in the world.

The commission to proclaim the gospel to the nations begins with Jesus' command of His disciples before His ascension into heaven, we find it in the gospel of *Mark (16:15);*

*"Go into all the world and proclaim
the gospel to the whole creation."*

The gospel, meaning Good News, was the message of salvation from sin and death through Christ's death and resurrection. It is the proclamation that His kingdom had come among us. The Gospel Message is so deep that we may never fully grasp its depth but is also simple enough for any child to grasp.

In essence the message of the gospel can be summed up as; God who created you and loves you, wants a restored relationship with you but your sin, which is offensive to God, must be dealt with in order for this reconciliation. God sent His son Jesus, to pay the price to free you from your sins, His son, Jesus, overcome the power of sin over you by giving his life on the cross, willingly laying down his own life for yours. His sacrifice has now paid the debt you owed and sin no longer has a claim over you. Jesus rose again on the third day, so he didn't only overcome sin but he also overcame death. All who call on Jesus as their lord and choose to follow Him, receive the gift of God's grace and are forgiven their sin. Jesus who has gone to prepare an eternal home for you, He will return for you and all His people, raise you up to be with him and you will live together with him for all eternity. He will also give you His Holy Spirit, to comfort you, lead you into truth, protect you, heal you, strengthen you and empower you to live a life pleasing to God while you wait for His return.

When we consider all that God has done for us 'Good news' seems such an understatement! The gospel is not just good news, it is the greatest, most powerful news. Jesus' disciples understood this. They loved the gospel message and they spread it wherever they went even at the cost of their own lives. Likewise, as we learn to understand the power and vast reaching effect of the gospel will find a deepening desire to make this message known to mankind.

In *Matthew (24:14)* we read;

> *"And this gospel of the kingdom will be proclaimed throughout the whole world as a testimony to all nations, and then the end will come."*

Jesus told His disciples that He would not come again until the Gospel had been proclaimed in all The earth. Incredibly in 21st century there are still parts of the earth that haven't heard the gospel. They are waiting on us who have already heard and believe to come and tell them.

In *Romans (10:12-16)* the question is posed "how will people hear the gospel?";

*"For there is no distinction between Jew and Greek;
for the same Lord is Lord of all, bestowing his
riches on all who call on him. For "everyone who
calls on the name of the Lord will be saved.
How then will they call on him in whom they
have not believed? And how are they to believe in
him of whom they have never heard? And how are
they to hear without someone preaching?
And how are they to preach unless they are sent?
As it is written, "How beautiful are the feet
of those who preach the good news!""*

The answer comes down to the sending of mes-
sengers, so great is the message that they bring
that we are told that their feet are considered
beautiful because they carried the message. This
passage is refreshing to you and me, we are the
ones that have been sent with the great message
of salvation. People will not hear the good news
unless we rise up and go with the message we
have been given.

As Christians we are followers of Jesus, we are to
do the things He did and obey the commandments
He gave us.

What did Jesus do? He proclaimed the gospel of
the kingdom!

What did Jesus command us to do? To take His gospel to all of creation!

The barriers to evangelism
So what stops us fulfilling our mission to preach the gospel message?

1. It's Difficult
There is no hiding the fact that serving God is not always easy. Sharing the gospel is a challenge and at times can just feel too difficult. That cannot be a reason to not engage with the work of sharing Christ's message. If it all seems too difficult to you, ask yourself "am I serious about my faith and am I committed to serving Christ, obeying His call to take the gospel to the ends of the earth or am I just looking for what I can get out of the Christian faith?" It's important for us to understand that alongside the blessing of being a follower of Christ is a call to lay down our lives as Christ lay down His life for us.

In *2 Timothy (2:3)* Paul tells Timothy to;

> *"Share in suffering as a good
> soldier of Christ Jesus."*

A life of service to God in the power of the Holy Spirit is the most exciting life that can be lived. When I look back at the adventures God has taken me on and the great joy I have had at seeing his kingdom growing on the earth it fills me with true happiness. Serving God wholeheartedly and obediently, means that we share in Christ's joy but also in His sufferings. It also means that we will go through times of sorrow and trial and this is where many Christians back away from His call. If we truly live for Christ then we will have to obey the words of *Matthew (16:24);*

> *"Then Jesus told his disciples, "If anyone would come after me, let him deny himself and take up his cross and follow me."*

Truly following Jesus means choosing to take up my cross. I have to learn to deny myself many of the things that I desired, because I want to be holy and pleasing to God. I probably fail as often as I succeed but I press on to be pleasing to God. When we look back times of victory through obedience can bring us joy, we celebrate that we did the right thing and honoured God but in the moment that choice could have been a real battle. Choosing to deny ourselves isn't enjoyable. It can feel like a heavy load to bear.. It would be so much easier to just do as we please, but we want to be a pleasing aroma to our God so we choose to do what honours Him rather than what pleases us. *Lamentations (3:17)* tells us that;

> *"It is good for a man that he bear the yoke in his youth."*

The kingdom of God brings us great joy and true satisfaction but there are also times of suffering and pain. I have a calling on my life to preach and minister to the nations. This has been confirmed to me time and time again through many prophetic words, scriptures and visions. It excites me and I love bringing good news to people around the world. I love meeting people of different cultures and I love seeing God move in people's lives bringing them healing and freedom. But alongside the joy and excitement comes trials and testing. Being a bearer of the gospel means that we will have difficult times.

This was brought home to me some time ago when I was returning from a mission trip to the Congo. I had been working with a Congolese friend setting up a ministry to teenage prostitutes. We sent out the church members to invite any young girls on the street to come to a meeting where we would give them lunch and pamper them for the afternoon, ladies from the church painted their nails and treated their hair. It was so exciting the next day as the girls came in, were fed and given bags of goodies. We shared the gospel with the girls and prayed with them. The church was to follow on with a training course to try and help them get off the streets and into education or work. I was so excited to be a part in this ministry but a few days later I would feel very differently. I had been wearing flip-flops all through the trip as the weather was very hot in Brazzaville. I didn't put my trainers on until the flight home. By the time I had arrived in the UK I was in terrible pain. I hadn't realised that my feet, which had swollen up on the plane, were covered in insect bites. I had had to put my trainers on to leave the plane and every step I took was incredibly painful. I walked from the plane to the train station fighting back tears. "God" I prayed "why do I have to go through this, it's so painful I can hardly stand up. I've been serving you, doing good work. Surely this is not right that I should suffer". If it hadn't been so cold I would have walked bare foot. As I moved and complained I felt God say to me. "This is what true mission feels like." The same point has been brought home to me again and again as I have got more involved in mission work.

One of my greatest joys is the work I am involved in serving God through mission work in Africa, this work though, does sometimes come at a cost. In my late teens and early twenties after spending time in Africa I developed a stomach problem that caused me great discomfort. It took nearly three years before my stomach returned to normal. Three times on returning from trips to Africa I have ended up in hospital. I have had food poisoning at least 7 times while in Africa and India. Ministry is not always easy and we can go through great pain while serving God. In our work in Zambia we have lost staff to HIV and accidents. My heart has been broken again and again as I have worked with people in extreme poverty. At points I have felt I can't bear it anymore, "it is too hard Lord, my heart can't keep breaking like this". I remember praying once. On a few occasions I have looked at the growth in our projects and been overwhelmed by the number of people that rely on us for care, food and housing. This work is not for the weak of heart. But God is always faithful and gives us the strength we need to go on. When I listen to the stories of others that have lost loved ones, been imprisoned, tortured and cast out of their families, I realise my suffering for the gospel is nothing in comparison with what my brothers and sisters in Christ have been through. I had one friend that was martyred in India, for preaching the gospel. Any sufferings or hardships we face, fade into insignificance when we see the greatness of God at work in the lives of men and women responding to the power of the gospel. I can look back and count these trials as joy now, when I see lives rescued and changed by the love of God. They are a small price to pay for the blessing of God working in and through my life.

In reality it is no sacrifice to serve Christ as the reward we receive is vastly greater than anything we lay down for him. One day Peter said to Jesus that he and the other disciples had left everything to follow him. In *Luke (18:29-30)*, we find Jesus' response to Peter;

"And he said to them, "Truly, I say to you,
there is no one who has left house or
wife or brothers or parents or children,
for the sake of the kingdom of God,
who will not receive many times more in this
time, and in the age to come eternal life.""

How incredible that Jesus promised to bless us with much more than we have sacrificed to follow him, both in this life and the one to come. Suffering for Christ brings reward that make our sufferings fade away in comparison. Christ suffered and died for us. Most of us will never be called to the challenge of losing loved ones or risking our lives to let others know of Christ's love for them. The most that we will face is a snigger or being called names. Yet we still choose not to put ourselves out for the gospel. If we are to be true disciples of Christ we must stop running from hardships, swallow our pride and start sharing the good news. When I consider the challenge of sharing the gospel with my family and friends it is no real burden in comparison to what many Christians go through on a daily basis. The church needs to take its calling to be ambassadors of Christ seriously.

Take Action
If you feel you are apathetic about the ministry of proclaiming the gospel or you feel ashamed to confess Christ, spend some time praying through

this issue. Ask God to forgive you for not taking His call seriously. Ask Him to place a passion in your heart to reach the lost. Ask for a boldness to come upon you. Begin to see yourself as a soldier in Christ's army. You exist for His will and glory.

2. Cares of this world

Returning to Paul's teaching in *2 Timothy (2:4)*, he continues;

> *"No soldier gets entangled in civilian*
> *pursuits, since his aim is to please*
> *the one who enlisted him."*

So often we can become consumed with 'civilian pursuits', unimportant and foolish things, that take our focus off the call to proclaim the gospel. It is not unheard of for churches to split over quarrels and disagreements that should be totally irrelevant to the people of Christ. We can become consumed by making our churches a safe, friendly, unchallenging place where we try to make sure that no one will ever be offended or challenged beyond their comfort zone. Our commitment to provide care and activities for every demographic of the church can eat up our time and resources to the degree that no time is left for seeking to make Christ known among the lost. Many churches focus on caring for their flock can lead them to neglect the equally important duty of proclaiming the gospel to the lost.

A good soldier is preoccupied in doing the work he has been given, he is not distracted by civilian things. Paul isn't saying that civilian things are not needed or are unimportant just that they should not entangle us and interfere with our mission. We must choose that our worldly cares will not hinder us from the call to reach the lost with the gospel.

Jesus told us in the parable of the Sower and the seed that the cares of this world choke the life away from believers. It can be so easy to lose sight of what God has called us to, because the cares of this world took over.

In my dream one of the reasons for not going out into the fire were due to 'cares and concerns'. There was concern that those of us that went might be hurt or that we might bring something bad into the house. We mustn't let 'cares and concerns' stop us from doing what we are called to do. Imagine if the disciples had said we can't go preach the gospel because we may be beaten or killed. No, we cannot let fear and cares hold us back from doing the work God has called us to.

One of the greatest lessons I have learned in life is that as I seek to please God and to do the things he has called me to do, he takes care of me. Jesus made this beautiful truth clear to us when he told his disciples;

Matt 6:25-33

""Therefore I tell you, do not be anxious about your life, what you will eat or what you will drink, nor about your body, what you will put on. Is not life more than food, and the body more than clothing? Look at the birds of the air: they neither sow nor reap nor gather into barns, and yet your heavenly Father feeds them. Are you not of more value than they? And which of you by being anxious can add a single hour to his span of life? And why are you anxious about clothing? Consider the lilies of the field, how they grow: they neither toil nor spin, yet I tell you, even Solomon in all his glory was not arrayed like one of these. But if God so clothes the grass of the field, which today is alive and tomorrow is thrown into the oven, will he not much more clothe you, O you of little faith? Therefore, do not be anxious, saying, 'What shall we eat?' or 'What shall we drink?' or 'What shall we wear?' For the Gentiles seek after all these things, and your heavenly Father knows that you need them all. But seek first the kingdom of God and his righteousness, and all these things will be added to you."

The cares of this world keep us from seeking the cares of the kingdom of God. Jesus taught us that rather than to be consumed by the very real needs of this life, we should focus on doing what pleases the Father and trust that he in turn will make sure we have the things we need. This isn't a license to ignore our responsibility to work and provide for our families but it is an invitation to prioritise God's kingdom over our own needs and wants, knowing that as we do so God will take care of those needs. I have experienced this supernatural provision over and over again in my life as I have chosen to walk according to the principles of the kingdom and prioritise Gods desires over my own. I have seen the lord provide homes, cars, finances in difficult times and even holidays when we have been unable to afford them. I will share just one example here.

The work I am involved in in Africa, means that I travel out to visit the projects around 3 times a year. While most of the cost of these trips is covered by a very generous church, not all the costs are covered and I often incur personal costs due to the travelling, also my family graciously allow me to leave them for two to three weeks every three or four months. This is a sacrifice they and I make because we see the work we are doing as 'seeking the kingdom'. It is a real sacrifice for my wife to let me go and have to manage the home and the children as well as cover some of my workload in my absence. It is a sacrifice for my children to not have their father at home for this time too. Some years ago as a church we planned a trip to Zambia to see the work we are doing out there. My wife and I felt that we should go on this trip with our children, so that they would see the work and know what it was that daddy was doing when he went off to Africa. Unfortunately, we had no money to pay for our trip. As we prayed, we both felt it was right for us to go on the trip as a family and so in faith we agreed to go. We began to tell friends and family that we were going to go but never mentioned that we didn't have the funds needed. Soon after a friend in our church approached us and said that they felt God leading them to give us some money each month for the next year. We put the money aside each month toward the cost of the flights. About 3 months later my friend Bunty came to visit. She had been in New Zealand and passed through Singapore on her way back to the UK. When we met she gave me $1,000 Singapore dollars. "What's this?" I asked. Bunty explained to me that a friend of mine in Singapore that I had met 20 years before had met her while she was there and given her the money to give to me. I hadn't seen or spoken to this friend for at least 15 years. "Is it for our work in Zambia?" I asked, "No, it's a personal gift for you." I was amazed. God had touched this friends heart to give this gift. My wife and I thanked God and continued to trust him for the rest of the funds needed for the trip. A few months later another gift of $1,000 came from Singapore. We now had the funds to cover all our flights. About a month before we were due to travel to Zambia, some old friends came to visit. We shared with them the amazing story of God's provision for this trip. We made no mention of our need to cover other costs. About a week later this wonderful couple send us a gift of several hundred British pounds. We had now covered all the expenses for the trip. From having nothing and without having to set aside any of our monthly income God had provided all the funds needed for our family of 5 to travel to Africa for 3 weeks. Praise God. A few days before we left a couple in our church gave us another gift toward our trip. It was enough to cover every extra expense on our trip, from ice creams to visiting an elephant orphanage. Without letting anyone know our need, we witnessed God's complete provision of our need and our wants. We had been truly blessed.

Seek first the kingdom and God will provide.

3. Comfort
Maybe the number one reason for us not being passionate about sharing the gospel is that we are too comfortable? When our comfort becomes more important to us than the lost being reached with the love of Christ, then it is time to radically shake things up, the church is not called to be comfortable but to obey Christ.

In my dream some of the people in the loft didn't want to bring in strangers or the wounded because they feared they would overcrowd the space we had and possibly bring in sickness, polluting our pure environment. This might sound like a ridiculous idea. What kind of church doesn't want people to come in. This would sound ridiculous to me if I hadn't witnessed it myself. I remember once going to a multi church function at which we were put into small groups with people from different churches. I was asked to lead a group which had a number of people from four different churches in it. Over the course of the evening our conversation turned to worship in church services and one couple in my group remarked how they had once been to a meeting where there had been drums playing in the worship time. "I wouldn't stay in a church that allowed drums and guitars, that's not true worship" said the husband. I was shocked at this man's attitude. He wasn't willing to have his church services adapt so as to be appealing to a different generation or demographic. He was more interested in what he liked and didn't like in his church service than engaging the lost. When a church is more bothered about maintaining its peaceful environment and keeping its people happy, than it is in bringing in the broken and wounded, then it becomes like a soldier that has forgotten their orders. It becomes tasteless salt. We are soldiers in God's army called to carry out his plans and purposes. The church is his instrument and should always be used for His purposes and pleasure not ours.

The good soldier wants to please his commander. Is our focus to please our commander and God or to please ourselves? In reality true lasting pleasure is only found in living lives pleasing to God. The earthly reword of self service is temporal and fading but the pleasure that comes from serving God brings reward in this life and the life to come. What is so wonderful is that as we seek first the pleasure of our Heavenly Father, He takes care of our earthly needs.

In my dream many in the attic were more concerned about keeping themselves and their home safe and clean, rather than in being good, obedient soldiers doing the will of their commander. We must always remember that what we have and who we are all belong to Jesus. We are here for him and for his will and desire.

True service to God requires sacrifice on the part of the servers along with a willingness to change and be changed. I believe much of the conflict and strife in our churches is due to its members living for themselves rather than for the advancement of the kingdom of God.

Truly reaching out with the gospel means getting messy and uncomfortable. It means sacrifice and self-denial. It means me feeling uncomfortable and out of my depth, but it leads to great joy and satisfaction.

4. Unbiblical doctrine

Another thing that keeps God's people from evangelising is wrong doctrine. There is a growing movement in many churches that teaches everyone will ultimately be saved, whether they accept Christ in this life or not. The argument goes that a loving God wouldn't send people to hell. I am shocked by how many "Christians" are toying with or embracing this doctrine. I understand why they are tempted to do so. Believing this lie makes the Christian Faith more palatable in a multi faith world where you are labelled an extremist if you hold to a complete biblical view. This view also makes us feel better about not sharing the gospel. 'It doesn't matter they will all go to heaven anyway.' To believe this kind of teaching though we must compromise and choose not to believe the teachings of Jesus Himself. At the beginning of this chapter we read *Mark (16:15)*, here it is again but this time with verse *16* added;

"And he said to them,
"Go into all the world and proclaim the gospel
to the whole creation. Whoever believes and is
baptised will be saved, but whoever does not
believe will be condemned."

Jesus makes it explicit that anyone who doesn't believe will be condemned. There is no scriptural basis for a universalist view and to believe it, you must deny the teachings of Christ. Read the Gospels and you will see for yourself. I believe the greatest hindrance to the advancement of the Gospel today is Christians who don't truly believe God's word.

Jesus taught that He would come again as a judge and that many would go into an eternal punishment. *Matt (25:41-46)* says;

> *"Then he will say to those on his left,*
> *depart from me, you cursed, into the eternal*
> *fire prepared for the devil and his angels.*
> *For I was hungry and you gave me no food,*
> *I was thirsty and you gave me no drink,*
> *I was a stranger and you did not welcome me,*
> *naked and you did not clothe me, sick and in*
> *prison and you did not visit me.'*
> *Then they also will answer, saying, 'Lord,*
> *when did we see you hungry or thirsty or a*
> *stranger or naked or sick or in prison, and did*
> *not minister to you?' Then he will answer them,*
> *saying, 'Truly, I say to you, as you did not do it to*
> *one of the least of these, you did not do it to me.'*
> *And these will go away into eternal punishment,*
> *but the righteous into eternal life.'"*

There is no doubt in my mind that if you choose to believe the universalist lie then you are proclaiming that Jesus was a liar. Which is it? Both can't be true! If there was no need to bring people to Christ through the proclamation of the gospel then Jesus is not just a liar but also a cruel master. He sent out His disciples and later Paul to proclaim this message and all of them were beaten, tortured and even executed for doing so. If there was no need then what kind of friend was He? Why allow your dearest friends to be treated like this if there was no need to proclaim the gospel message?

In some places we have become more concerned about our church buildings than about reaching the lost. I have seen beautiful church buildings in nations where half the people are struggling to survive living hand to mouth and often unable to feed their families. I sometimes wonder what Jesus would say to His church today. Would He even recognise us as His own? It's not wrong to have an attractive building, but how can we justify extravagance on a building and ignore the needs of God's own children. On the day when we stand before Christ for judgment and He says to us, "did you feed, clothe, wash, shelter or visit my brothers and sisters in need." I wonder if we were to reply, "no Lord I didn't but look I built you a really nice building." How would He respond?

Action Point
If you have believed this fake gospel then repent. Change your thinking. Ask God to forgive you for being misled by believing the thoughts and teaching of men over the teachings of Jesus and for not trusting God's word. Ask God to lead you in truth

and give you a better understanding of His gospel message.

5. Fear

In my dream one of the challenges in bringing in those in the fire was that they would contaminate our home. One danger the church faces is falling into the trap of believing that keeping our church building and people clean and safe is our greatest priority. We can become fearful of worldliness coming in, believing that if sinners come in among us they will lead the younger and weaker members of the church astray.

Another of the responses in my dream was fear for those of us that were going out to help, in case we got injured ourselves. It is interesting that often opposition to the church moving on and taking ground in evangelism comes from within the church itself. Fear must never dictate our decisions, fear is not from God. Knowing Christ's love enables us to overcome fear.

Maybe a more common fear though, is the fear of man or the fear of the world. Let me define what we mean by 'the World', I'm not talking about the planet we live on but rather the worldly system and mindset that seeks to dominate the thinking and behaviour of mankind. The kingdom, or kingdoms of this world are that which are at odds with the Kingdom of our Christ. The world is a system that often stands against the church. We have opposing reasons for existing. Jesus told us that people would hate us and try to silence us, so we know that the world will oppose us. The church lives for Christ while the world lives for itself. And yes, we know that proclaiming the gospel can bring persecution and opposition against us but as has already been said the trials we face are insignificant compared to the sufferings of Christ and the glory set before us.

John (3:16) tells us;

""For God so loved the world, that he gave his only Son, that whoever believes in him should not

perish but have eternal life."

Christ came (and died) because God loved the world. We need to be filled with God's love for the world so we can overcome fear and make Christ known. I live in a country where we are given relative freedom of speech. I'm not in danger of losing my life for sharing the gospel and yet I find I can be ashamed of confessing Christ. In the dream the negative words weren't from people who disliked us! They were the voices of well-meaning friends who didn't want to see us hurt. Fear from within the church can hold us back from proclaiming the gospel. We need to be a people who listen and respond to what God tells us to do.

Isaiah (43:2) says;

> *"When you pass through the waters,*
> *I will be with you; and through the rivers,*
> *they shall not overwhelm you; when you walk*
> *through fire you shall not be burned,*
> *and the flame shall not consume you."*

We can walk through the fire and water and it will not harm us. Why should we be afraid of the world when we have Christ with us?

Take Action
If you are fearful of sharing your faith with others, begin to ask God to overcome that fear in you with boldness. Ask him to give you opportunities to share about him with your loved ones and neighbours. Ask God to give you a confidence in the bible and in the power of the gospel. Read books about and listen to testimonies of people who came to Christ, learn what was done that caused this conversion. Ask the Holy Spirit to show you what to say and do.

The challenge for the church in our day, is to rediscover the importance of proclaiming the gospel to the lost, we must again become the ones who give shelter, food and love to those in need in Jesus' name. We must overcome fear of man and walk in the fear of the Lord. Please don't take me for someone that thinks the church is all wrong and does no good. I am so encouraged by the incredible work that local churches do both in the UK and around the world. Churches feed, cloth, house and love all sorts of people. They counsel couples struggling in their marriages, they care for children from broken families, they pray for those in need and they give so generously. All of this is beautiful and honouring to the names of Jesus. The challenge is that in all this good we do, we must not neglect to tell people the gospel message.

Some years ago, I was in India on a mission trip with a few friends. We were ministering at evening rallies and teaching church leaders at day conferences. One of the speakers was an Indian man who was being used mightily in gifts of healing and miracles. On our journey to a town we were going to have our meetings in this brother sat in the front of the car speaking to the Hindu driver, after about 20 minutes he began to speak and the driver repeated what he said. I realised that he was leading the man in a prayer of repentance. The driver then wiped away a mark he had on his forehead, which he had worn as a sign of commitment to his gods. As we drove through a toll booth the paster encouraged the man to confess his faith and the driver told the tollbooth attendant that Jesus was Lord. I was blessed by the simplicity of how our friend led this man to the Lord. We soon stopped for a drink at a service station and our friend shared the gospel with the worker in the shop. This man too, committed his life to the Lord. We were traveling in convoy and so our friend was asked to move to the other car to speak to that driver also. By the time we had arrived at our destination, this driver too, had committed his life to the Lord.

This was such an awesome thing to witness but it was hard for me and my friends to accept. Had these people really made a true commitment? Could we really expect them to change after such a short encounter? As I thought about these things, I was reminded of all the people that met with Jesus. Their lives were changed in a moment. I had also been a little concerned that our friend the Indian evangelist, may have put pressure on these people to accept Christ. As I thought about it, I realised where I was. These men had possibly never heard the truth about Jesus before, they were lost in idolatry and needed freedom. My friend was doing all he could to save them from their sin and to bring them to the living Saviour. I began to feel convicted about my wrong thinking. Why has sharing the gospel become so alien to me? Why don't I urge people to receive Christ? Am I ashamed of my saviour? People do change after such a short encounter and we as God's children should not be shocked or doubtful that there is a lasting effect in their lives.

We have become so used to thinking that people need a great amount of time to choose Christ, we are afraid that people will think we are pushing them into making a decision. How interesting it would have been if Jesus thought that way. Can you imagine him going to Peter, John or any of the other disciples and saying to them; "I want you to think about maybe coming with me. No rush, don't be hasty in making a decision you may regret, just think about it and if you decide you would like to then here's my card, come visit me." I don't think so. "Come follow me." That's what he said and that's what they did. We make it so hard for people to receive salvation, when God has done all he can to make it so easy. We need to return to the purpose that God called us too! To know Him and make Him known. Are we willing to put aside our comfort and go where he says and do what he asks us to do?

The book of Joshua gives us a great picture of how God wants to move through his people. Joshua and the Israelites took the promised land before them, not by might nor by power but by the spirit of the Lord. It was God who caused Jericho to fall. It was God that gave His people victory time and time again in battle over their enemy. However, God used the hands, feet, trumpets and swords of the Israelites to do it. I don't for one minute think that the Israelites enjoyed the work. Battle was a scary, messy and tiresome place. Some of the demands God had put on his people were difficult and horrifying to carry out. The Israelites were not to leave anyone alive. Put yourself in their place. You have to kill men, women and children. I don't think it was an ethnic cleansing rampage, fuelled by racial hatred stirred up by demonic forces. It was obedience to God, and maybe the hardest thing the Israelites would be asked to do. The power the people had was in their obedience to the call of God. As long as they walked in the love and fear of the Lord they had the victory. What an awesome picture this is of us working with the Holy Spirit in our lives. We need to move away from the idea that Christ came to give me a good life, to make me rich and happy. Where it is true that the work of Jesus is for our ultimate blessing and that God desires to meet all our needs, to show fatherly love to us and to pour his abundance on us the deeper truth is that he has accepted us to be his children and his servants. This is the greatest treasure we could ever receive.

We were created for God's pleasure. As a Christian I have to learn to embrace the truth that I am not my own. I belong to God. *1 Corinthians (6:19-20)* tells us that we are not our own and that we were bought with a great price. That price that was paid for us was the Christ himself and there is no more valuable thing in all of creation. In the same way our local church does not belong to the members that make up the congregation but each and every Christian church belongs to Christ. We, the church are His body and He is our head (*Colossians 1:17-18)*. Our role then, as the body of Christ, is to carry out his desires here in the world. So when he says go, we go. When he says love, we love.

There is a world to be won for Christ and we, the church, are the body He has chosen to work through to reach this world.

Empowered by the Spirit
The beautiful thing is that God doesn't tell us to do what he will not empower us to do. His power works through us to do his will. In my dream not only were we unharmed by the fire but we were able to bring healing and restoration into lives that had been ravaged by the fire and who in the natural had no hope. The same spirit living in us, raised Christ from the dead! If we are willing to follow his lead then he will do great works through us. If we will listen to the voice of the spirit, look for opportunity to meet the needs of others and be willing to step outside of our comfort zone, then we can expect to see God use us for great works.

All that we can do for Christ is dependent on us being willing and ready to be used. Often I find I am more willing than I am ready. I want to be used by God but I have done little to prepare myself for the engagement I am entering into.

We can be better prepared for reaching the world with the gospel message by building ourselves up spiritually. This building up is done in prayer and in studying scripture. It is the Holy Spirit that empowers me and so I need to invest time and energy in letting the Holy Spirit's power and influence grow inside of me.

In *1 Tim (2: 1-4)* Paul tells us;

> *"First of all, then, I urge that supplications,
> prayers, intercessions, and thanksgivings be
> made for all people, for kings and all who are
> in high positions, that we may lead a peaceful
> and quiet life, godly and dignified in every way.
> This is good, and it is pleasing in the sight of God
> our Saviour, who desires all people to be saved
> and to come to the knowledge of the truth."*

God desires all people to be saved and come to the
knowledge of the truth. This then needs to become our desire also. In the same passage Paul
tells Timothy that the church is to pray for all
people. It is the duty of the church to reach the
lost through prayer and proclamation of the gospel. There is a world of people lost in their sin,
needing the church to reach them with the power
of the gospel.

Called to be Salt and Light
The house in my dream represents the church.
The church is not a building but the people of God.
These people are made up of believers from all
over the world. It is important that we understand
that the bible uses the term 'church' to define the
global church which is the one people of God in

the earth but it also uses the word church to talk about a local group of Christians that meet together to worship, pray and receive teaching from the scriptures. This local church is both a part of the global church and yet distinct. We can understand this in the way that we understand that our bodies are made up of cells. Our cells are part of our body and in fact the body wouldn't be here without the cells. However a cell on its own is not a body and should a cell die the body continues without it and even creates new cells to replace the dead ones. As a Christian I am part of the body, but I also need to be part of one of the cells that make up this body.

Each local church is different to other churches due to the people in it and the affiliation it has with other groups of churches. There can be beauty in these diversities, and we find different strengths and weaknesses in different structures and denominations. What is vital though is that each local group of Christians (church), lives out its devotion to God as He instructs us. Churches must not become clubs of like-minded people, wishing to maintain the status quo and unwilling to break from tradition if we find it is not in line with the teaching of scripture. It is possible for a group of Christians to be more concerned about protecting their church traditions than in walking out the call that God has given to His church, particularly the call to take the gospel message of the world. Jesus tells us in *Matthew (5:13-14);*

"You are the salt of the earth,
but if salt has lost its taste,
how shall its saltiness be restored?
It is no longer good for anything except to
be thrown out and trampled under people's feet.
You are the light of the world.
A city set on a hill cannot be hidden."

Salt is an amazing substance. As well as adding taste it can be used for many things, including cleansing and preserving. When Jesus declared that we are salt, He was expressing to us that we are not powerless but that we are a substance that can change the world. However, Jesus warns us that if the salt isn't salty it is worthless.

This passage gives us a challenge and a great way of measuring the effectiveness of a local church. As a church do people know we are there because they recognise a distinct flavour in us? Are we as local churches, shining a light into the darkness? Salt has a very distinct taste that is easily recognised. Jesus is telling his followers that if they are to truly be what he has called them to be then they must be distinct from the world around them. As followers of Jesus we should leave a distinct flavour. It is an obvious point to make but as a Christian my words and deeds should be like Christ's. That's what Christian means, Christ One, one who is like Christ. Jesus was the distinctly different flavour that came into the world and we as his disciples bring his unique distinct flavour to mankind. Salt loses its taste when it has become contaminated with something else making its flavour weak or unpleasant. When we remove or dilute the teachings of Christ and the presence of the Holy Spirit from our churches, then our flavour is no longer distinct and Christ filled but rather becomes weak and ineffective. When we mix the world in with Christ the salt becomes contaminated, and the taste becomes unpleasant to the world around us and much more so to our Father God.

The church is called to be a distinct flavour in the world. If we interact with the world around us but have no distinct taste then we are no longer fit for purpose. All we are good for is to be thrown out. What a huge challenge to the church in a day when many want the church to become more worldly. If a local church loses or ignores its mandate to reach the lost for Christ then it becomes like tasteless salt. It may be big and loud and look attractive to others but in God's economy it is worthless.

Being the "salt of the earth" means that we are to be in the world, tasted by people, bringing the flavour of God to them.

In the same way Jesus told His followers that they were "the light of the world". As Jesus' followers today, we are meant to shine before all men, not to be hidden away. It is impossible to remain hidden when we live out the call of God to take his gospel to the nations of the earth.

We are not meant to push our faith (belief in Jesus) on people, like some unwanted medication but rather we are to "let our good deeds shine" so that the world will see them and glorify our Father in heaven. Jesus, who is always our model for life, never hid his faith (belief in God). In fact, His confession and demonstration of faith caused him to be exposed to the multitudes from all walks of life. His faith caused him to be exposed to questioning and criticism by both the common people and the religious scholars. His faith caused him to be exposed on a cross, naked and alone. If Christ is our example, then keeping our faith private is not an option for us to consider.

If the church is not proclaiming Christ then we are not walking in the calling that God has given us. We are to "go into all the world and make disciples". If we hide away from challenges and dangers rather than facing them, we will never do the work God has called us to. God gives us gifts to enable us to reach a needy world with all that they need, to bring healing, to set free the captives and most importantly to bring people to salvation through the proclamation of the gospel.

As Christians, we receive the Holy Spirit into our lives, therefore we carry God's presence with us wherever we go. To put it another way, God is present with us at all times. This isn't like carrying a picture of God on our phone with us. God is actually with us. At times we are more aware of this fact than at others but he is always here no matter what we feel.

Jesus said to his disciples that they, (and so by extension, also you and I) are the light of the world. This light is the answer to the darkness that mankind finds itself in. Whilst we can save no one by our own power we are the light that illuminates the way to Christ. We shine and allow people to walk in truth. We are Salt and Light. We have all that a lost world needs to find hope and life. The challenge for us is; will we give ourselves to be used by God to bring that salt and light to those who need it. A lost world cannot afford for us to have a private faith that is kept hidden from others. True faith is active, it must be lived out for all to see. We are not to hide our light away but let it shine out into the darkness showing people a more excellent way lighting a path for people to come into the family of God.

Keys to effective evangelism
So how can we embrace this call to reach the lost and be more affective in evangelism? Maybe like me you have tried to be a better evangelist but each time you try you soon run out of steam or

lose the passion. I believe with all my heart that all that what God calls us to He equips us for. Let's consider some ways we can become more effective in the ministry of evangelism.

1.Understand the gospel

First of all we need to understand what the gospel message is. In *1 Peter (3:15)*, Peter tells us;

> *"but in your hearts honor Christ the Lord*
> *as holy, always being prepared to make a*
> *defence to anyone who asks you for a reason*
> *for the hope that is in you; yet do it with*
> *gentleness and respect,"*

We are told to be ready to give an account for what we believe. If we don't understand the need or importance of the gospel then we will never feel the need to share it with the world. Choose to make it a priority to understand the gospel message.

The gospel is the hope of all mankind. By it we find forgiveness (*1 John 2:2*), salvation (*Ephesians 2:8*) and the hope of eternal life (*1 Peter 1:3-5*). One thing that has helped me to develop to better grasp God's truths from scripture is to choose to meditate upon it. Sit and think about what Jesus has done for you through His death on the cross and his resurrection from the dead. If you are in a position of church leadership, challenge your church to develop a deeper understanding of the gospel message. I believe if we truly understood the gospel and taught the gospel to our churches then we would create a people with a passion to reach the lost with the love of Jesus.

Make sharing the gospel a priority

Next, we have to make sharing the gospel a priority. Don't think of sharing the gospel as something only evangelists can do but embrace that as a child of God and follower of Jesus, you are called to make Him known in the earth. You are called to proclaim the gospel. It is not a matter of if you will share it but how you will share it. If the thought of sharing your faith is a difficult one for you then take some time to sit and write down why you are a Christian, what the gospel message is and how it's affected your life. Consider the sharing of the gospel as part of your devotion to Christ. In church services make it a priority to explain the gospel and invite people to respond to it regularly.

3. Seek empowerment

When Jesus left His disciples and ascended into heaven, He gave them instructions on what they should do next. They were to go into Jerusalem and wait for the Holy Spirit to come upon them. As it says in *Acts (1:4-5);*

> *"And while staying with them he ordered them not to depart from Jerusalem, but to wait for*

the promise of the Father, which, he said,
"you heard from me; for John baptized
with water, but you will be baptized with
the Holy Spirit not many days from now.""

Jesus' disciples had heard His teachings, they had known His friendship and they had witnessed His miracles, but something was still missing. Before they were ready to begin the work of proclaiming the gospel they needed one more thing. They needed the empowerment that came through the baptism of the Holy Spirit. God hasn't called us to make Christ known to the world through our testimony and our works alone. He has called us to make Christ known through lives empowered by the Holy Spirit. Jesus' instructions to His disciples are so important for us to understand. We, like them, are not called to serve God in our own strength but in God's strength. The ministry of the Church to make Christ known to every people, tribe and tongue is not possible in our own strength, but by the power of the Holy Spirit working in and through us, we are able to see the impossible happen.

This has been shown true time and time again throughout church history. In the first few hundred years of the church, there arose great opposition to Christianity. Persecution from individuals and from the state sought to blot out the church from the earth. Somehow though the church wasn't blotted out, rather in those seasons it grew all the more. The same phenomenon has been observed in Communist China. On the 19 Apr 2014, the Telegraph, a prominent British newspaper published an article entitled "China on course to become 'world's most Christian nation' within 15 years". The article said that it is predicted that by 2030 China's total Christian population, would exceed 247 million, placing it above Mexico, Brazil and the United States as the largest Christian congregation in the world. This in a nation that is known to have locked up Christians for sharing their faith. It is not just China. The same thing is happening in many Muslim nations. Countries where once it was nearly impossible to find Christians are finding more and more that people are turning to faith in Jesus Christ. How is this possible when the culture and government are opposed to Christians sharing their faith? It is possible because the Holy Spirit is at work through the lives of God's people. There is no government, no belief system and no religion that can prevent the Holy Spirit doing His work through Jesus' disciples. This is why Jesus' disciples had to wait for the Holy Spirit, because it is the work of the spirit that brings people to salvation. If we wish to be effective evangelists then we need the empowering that comes from the Holy Spirit.

The wonderful news is that God wants to fill us with His Holy Spirit even more than we want Him to. If we can learn to seek God to fill us with His anointing and power then we can be well equipped for the ministry of bringing others to faith. We are not meant to just rush out with the good news but rather to be filled by the Holy Spirit and partner with Him as He directs us to those that are seeking the truth.

4. Pray

Fourthly we must pray, pray and pray. The work of winning souls is a spiritual work. Sometimes we are battling spiritual forces that would blind those we are seeking to win. We need to pray for the lost to find Christ, pray for our churches to understand the importance of sharing the gospel and pray for ourselves that we would be filled and led by the spirit to those that we can bring to Christ.

5. Go

Finally if we are to be effective evangelists then we must act. The disciples once they were filled with the Holy Spirit had to get up and do something. They had to engage their community with the Gospel message. This was done initially by them leaving the upper room and going out into the streets, going where the people were. We likewise have to go where the people are, sharing honestly the gospel message as we care for those in need in Christs name, pray for people's physical, emotional, material and spiritual needs. Whatever we do one thing is necessary; we have to Go. The church must get back to its call to proclaim the gospel. We must once again tell people what the gospel is and how they can receive it in their lives.

Action Point
If you, like me, have struggled to be engaged in evangelism, then acknowledge this before God. Ask Him to change you, to give you a love for the lost. Ask Him to give you opportunity to share the gospel with others. Ask the Holy Spirit to come into your life more and more. Ask him to give you God's heart for evangelism and to demonstrate the power of God through your life as signs accompanying the proclamation of the gospel

Offer prayer
One very simple way we can share the gospel is by offering to pray for people. By offering prayer we do three things. We tell the person that we believe in God, that we care about them and we create an opportunity for the Holy Spirit to move in the person's life, revealing to them that He is real. I have found that offering to pray for someone is the best way to begin to share the gospel with them. You don't have to push your opinions on them just be a channel and often they will then ask you why you believe what you believe.

Confirmation
When I returned home from the Czech Republic a week after receiving this dream, a friend of mine told me that there had been a fire the week before near my parents' house in France. My brother had

woken in the night and went out of the caravan where he was staying in the garden. As he stepped outside he began to smell smoke and see flames rising above our forest. My brother woke the family and my parents immediately telephoned the fire brigade whilst getting everyone out of the house and into the cars, ready to evacuate. My father and another elder from our church stood in front of the house and prayed for Gods protection over the property. The fire fighters fought the fire through the night and by morning the fire was out. Later that week, my family had gone to look at the damage. They discovered that the fire had burned right to the edge of our forest down two sides but not one of our trees had been burned. It seems that the wind had been blowing the fire toward our house, but at the time when it was about to hit our land, the same time my family were praying, the wind changed direction. I was amazed that although I had no knowledge of this happening, I had been dreaming of a fire outside our home that was unable to touch our house. Of course, the time and manner that God speaks to us is never a coincidence. Had I had this dream any other time, it would have still impacted me greatly, but to find days later that my dream was a near mirror of what was actually happening brought home to me the depth and importance of what God was saying to me.

Prayer

Here is a prayer to help us seek God to work in us. Lord God, my Father, please give me Your heart for this world. Don't let me be so consumed with my own needs and wants, that I miss the whole point of why I am here. I am your servant. Do not let me deter my brothers and sisters from good works but let me encourage them in love and grace. Help me not to hide my salt away but pour me out over all the needs of the world around me. Give glory to your name through my words and deeds. May my love for you be evident in my service of others. Amen.

Summary

God has called his church to reach the world with the Gospel, the Gospel is the good news of the love of God made known through the offering of Christ for our sins. God desires to welcome us into his family and lead us in righteous living, inviting us to rule with him eternally. Many things will keep us from sharing the gospel with the world but we are to overcome these obstacles and make Christ known through sharing his gospel in word, deed and through a demonstration of the power of the Holy Spirit.

6. Conclusion
Final thoughts

3 John 1:4

"I have no greater joy than to hear
that my children are walking in the truth".

This book has taken me many years to complete. I have had to rewrite it's chapters many times. I've set deadlines that came and went over and over again. Finally, after nearly 30 years from the time I felt God prompt me to write a book of some the dreams he had given me here it is. I'm left asking myself "what benefit will it bring to those that read it?" I hope that its benefit will be twofold.

Firstly I hope that the dreams themselves will stick with the reader in the same way they have with me. That they will be like parables helping spiritual truths to be simply understood. Over the years these dreams have helped me to stay focused on what I believe God wanted to be a priority in my life and service. I hope that any reader of this book will likewise see God's heart and make the things that are important to Him, a priority in their own lives. In 3rd John (1:4) John tells Gaius, the recipient of his letter, that his greatest joy is to hear that his children are walking in truth. I can truly echo that sentiment. There would be no greater joy for me than to hear that what I have shared in this book has encouraged my Christian brothers and sisters to continue to walk in God's truth and to delve deeper in to the riches of His grace and love. In recent years my focus in ministry has shifted to teaching and training young leaders in Africa. Through Life Community Ministries we have established a number of churches in Zambia, Malawi and Mozambique. Our desire for these churches and their leaders is that they would go deeper and further in their knowledge and service of God than we who came before them. I hope that these dreams will be an encouragement to them all.

My second hope is that this book has created a hunger in the hearts of it's readers to hear from God themselves. It is one thing to teach someone what you have learned but a much greater thing to inspire others to pursue a deeper relationship with their heavenly Father. My greatest desire is that any reader of this book will call on God to speak to them, to show them his ways and teach them through his word and through the working of the Holy Spirit in their lives. In 1 Corinthians (14:1), Paul tells the Corinthians;

"Pursue love, and earnestly desire the spiritual gifts, especially that you may prophesy."

We likewise are to desire the spiritual gifts that come from God's Holy Spirt. I hope that this book has birthed a desire in its readers to hear from God in visions and dreams and that as a result, many more messages from God will be received, shared and bear fruit.

Thank you for taking the time to read this book. I do hope it has been a blessing to you.

Nathanael Edwards

About The Author:
Nathanael Edwards is Church Minister at Life Community Church Storrington. He lives in West Sussex, England, with his wife Katherine and their three children. His time is divided between working for Life Community Church and Life Support Charity. Nathanael has traveled extensively and visits Africa regularly, to oversee a number of projects that Life Support run there. He also helps to oversee the Life Community Ministries network of churches.

About Life Support:
Life Support is a charity registered in the UK and in the USA. It works to care for Orphans, widows and those suffering due to poverty and disabilities in developing nations.

If you would like to find out more about Life Support you can do so on our website www.lifesupportcharity.org

About Life Community Ministries:
Life Community Ministries is a family of churches in multiple nations working together to make Christ known in the earth.

If you would like more information on Life Community Ministries, please visit our website www.lifecommunityministries.org

Ingram Content Group UK Ltd.
Milton Keynes UK
UKHW021157220623
423873UK00015B/483